# CRACK CLAT & AILET [ENGLISH LANGUAGE SECTION]

## LAW ENTRANCE EXAMS PRACTICE SETS: ACCORDING TO THE LATEST SYLLABUS

DR PREETI TEWARI

Copyright © Dr Preeti Tewari
All Rights Reserved.

to all those who aspire to bring a change in the social framework by ensuring justice to all

# Contents

# Preface



The academic market is flooded with many books for guiding law aspirants. I will be failing in our duty if we don't justify writing yet another book- thereby adding to the already existing pool of books. For a while I've been pondering over the need to come up with a book that gives children/ youngsters/ law aspirants a clear cut solution to the problem of not having sufficient material to practice one of the toughest sections in the CLAT & AILET exams- English Language. We being the non native population, are always in serach of finding an appropriate and accurate collection of practice sets that help us better our language skills which decide our fate in terms of cracking the above mentioned renowned exams, thereby, ensuring a seat in the leading NLUs/ premier institutions of our country.

This is a fairly appropraitely carved out collection of 11 practice sets to begin with. The number has been decided to refrain from straining the children/ youngsters/ law aspirants. I feel that quality should supercede quantity and a fair amount of revision and reading exposure could prove to be a guarantee to good preparation.

The book adheres to the latest syllabus released by the Consortium of NLUs.

Looking forward to helping each one of you in the endeavour to better your comprehension skills w.r.t. the English Language section of the said exams.

*Happy Practising!*

Dr Preeti Tewari

# Acknowledgements

I am indebted to the following in the same order:-

1.  The Almighty
2.  My Parents
3.  My Friends
4.  My support system- My Gems- My students!!!


**Disclaimer:** I remain indebted to all those people/ sources that I have used in order to help the law aspirants in any which way.

In case, I missed mentioning any of the names/ sources then, I, hereby, express my sincere apologies and assure that I'm truly grateful to you/ the said source for letting me go ahead with the sacred job of helping law aspirants.

# CHAPTER ONE

# PRACTICE SET-1 [ENGLISH LANGUAGE]

# PASSAGE-1

Elections were in the air of the world's youngest democracy when I arrived in Thimphu. This was for a by-election in the capital city that dominated the conversation at dinners, even in Thimphu's most fun night-spot Mojo Park (the best music in town). Bhutan has taken to democracy with ease ever since 2008 when the first proper elections were held, a process India has helped out with, sending officials from the Election Commission travelling to check arrangements, explain electronic voting machine (EVM) technology and procedures.

Monks and nuns in this deeply religious Buddhist majority are not allowed to vote, so as to avoid mixing religion and politics. All voters must wear their national dress on polling day, but no one—candidate, campaigner or voter—is allowed to wear the kabney silk and gyentag (scarf of honour, for men and women respectively, bestowed only by the King), patang (ceremonial sword), or any other sign of rank or royal patronage to avoid a misuse of influence.

In Thimphu, the Textile Museum is run by the Royal Textile Academy - project of Ashi Sangay Choden Wangchuck, one of the Queen Mothers of Bhutan (the former King had four Queens, all sisters). The museum is dedicated to preserving the oldest and rarest woven fabrics worn in Bhutan and used in their religious **scrolls** and Thangkhas. As you walk in, it is the 'Thongdrel' or massive silk work of the Zhabdrung Phuensum Tshogpa (in honour of a sacred meal served to Bhutan's political and spiritual founder in 1637) that greets you. The thongdrel stands 34 feet tall, running 23 feet across and is set against a glass window that runs three stories high.

Tara Lakhang and Pangrizampa monastery on the **outskirts** of Thimphu is Bhutan's only monastery dedicated to 21 Taras, the female Bodhisattva and it is a powerful display of ancient feminism.

While polygamy is practiced in some parts, so is polyandry, and divorce settlements are equal and even-handed. Even so, Bhutanese women lag behind in one place that it counts: parliament. In the last National Assembly elections, 3/4ths of the 47 seats had only male candidates (nine had females), and four women were elected as MPs. "**Misogyny** plays only one part of it," explains the only leader of a party (DCT) Lily Wangchuk, who runs a hotel in downtown Thimphu. "Women just don't vote for women, and the lack of women role models in modern

Bhutan becomes a vicious cycle."

The Kyichu Lhakhang, in Paro, is one of Bhutan's oldest and simplest monasteries, believed to be constructed in 659 CE, by Tibetan king Songtsen Gampo.

All year round, one is welcomed into Kyichu with a spectacular and miraculous orange tree **laden** with fruit.

[**Source:** Extracted and Edited from The Hindu; April 01, 2017]

**1.1.** Which of the following statements is/are correct regarding the 2008 Elections of Bhutan?

I.   India helped Bhutan in elections by sending officials from Election Commission

of India.

I.   Monks and nuns were not allowed to vote.

II.   Wearing National Dress on Election Day was compulsory.

a.   I and II only

(b) II and III only

(c) I and III only

(d) All are Correct

**1.2.** Who is 'Ashi Sangay Choden Wangchuck' as mentioned in the passage?

(a) The elected Prime Minister of Bhutan

(b) The elected President of Bhutan

(c) Queen Mother of Bhutan

(d) None is Correct

**1.3.** Consider the following statements regarding the 'Mojo Park' as mentioned in the passage.

I. It is situated in the Northeast India

II. It is famous for its Music Shows

III. It is situated in the City of Thimphu

(a) All are Correct

(b) II and III only

(c) I and III only

(d) I and II only

**1.4.** Which of the following statements is correct as given in the Passage?
(a) Polyandry is not practiced in Bhutan
(b) Polygamy is practiced in Bhutan
(c) There is not a single Female Member in Bhutan's Parliament
(d) None is Correct

**1.5.** Why was candidate, campaigner or voter not allowed to wear any sign of rank or royal

patronage in the 2008 Elections of the country?
(a) Due to some kind of superstition.
(b) Due to some kind of superstition.
(c) To neglect the misuse of influence of wealthy and famous people
(d) None is Correct

**1.6.** Consider the following statements regarding the 'Kyichu Lhakhang' as given in the passage:
I. He was the first Prime Minister of Bhutan.
II. It is one of Bhutan's oldest monasteries.
III. It was built in 7th Century.

(a) I and II only
(b) II and III only
(c) I and III only
(d) None is Correct

**1.7.** Choose the word which is Most Similar to the word printed in bold in the passage

**Scrolls**
(a) Document
(b) Aimless
(c) Rolling
(d) None is Correct

**1.8.** Choose the word which is Most Similar to the word printed in bold in the passage.

**Outskirts**
(a) Periphery
(b) Center
(c) Downtown
(d) Away

**1.9.** Choose the word which is Most Opposite to the word printed in bold in the passage.

**Laden**
(a) Empty
(b) Full
(c) Charged
(d) Encumbered

**1.10.** Choose the word which is Most Opposite to the word printed in bold in the passage.

**Misogyny**
(a) Woman-hater
(b) Sexist
(c) Feminist
(d) None is Correct

# PASSAGE-2

Kabaddi has been one of the most underrated sports for long. Vivo Pro Kabaddi is a ground-breaking initiative by Mashal Sports Pvt. Ltd and Star India Pvt. Ltd. Ever since its **inception** in 2014, the League has revolutionised the sport of Kabaddi with stunning innovations, making it an inspirational sport for players and fans alike.

The league's inception was influenced by the popularity of the Kabaddi tournament at the 2006 Asian Games. The format of the competition was influenced by Indian Premier League. The Pro Kabaddi League uses a franchise-based model and its first season was held in 2014 with eight teams each of which having paid fees of up to US$250,000 to join.

Mashal Sports and STAR India have jointly worked towards elevating the sport of Kabaddi to an international standard with new and exciting innovations in the rules and how the game is viewed, thus heralding in a new **era** for Kabaddi. They infused new life into the sport by bringing it to the major metropolitan cities of India along with regions where Kabaddi was yet to gain a foothold. Vivo Pro Kabaddi now has unprecedented participation from various parts of the country owing to the outreach over the past seasons and the advent of new programmes pioneered by Mashal Sports to encourage young talent from across the country. Kabaddi is now also seen as a viable career option by various aspiring players in India and abroad.

There were doubts over whether the PKL would be successful, noting that there were many leagues attempting to **emulate** the IPL's business model and success, and that unlike cricket, there were relatively fewer well-known players in Kabaddi. However, it was also noted that Kabaddi was widely played in grassroots community settings, and could thus attract a wide variety of rural and metropolitan viewers for advertisers to target if the league gained significant traction.

The addition of four new teams in the fifth edition of the league made vivo Pro Kabaddi India's biggest sports league in terms of geographical representation and number of teams. The new sides – Gujarat Fortunegiants, Haryana Steelers, Tamil Thalaivas and U.P. Yoddha made the competition all the more **intense** and the Kabaddi all the more exciting.

The inaugural season was seen by 435 million viewers, Mashal sports placing it just behind the total-season viewership of the 2014 Indian Premier League season, while the inaugural championship was seen by 86.4 million viewers. Star Sports, the PKL's broadcaster, subsequently announced in 2015 that it would acquire a 74% stake in the league's parent company Mashal Sports.

For the 2017 season, the PKL added four new teams, and changed its format to split the teams into two divisions known as "zones".

[**Source:** Extracted and Edited from https://www.mbarendezvous.com/easy-reading-comprehension-passages/]

**2.1.** When was the professional Kabaddi league (PKL) started, who was the broadcast partner

and what is it currently called?

a.  2014, Start Sports, Vivo Pro Kabaddi League
(b) 2014, Zee Tv, Verizon Premier Kabaddi League
(c) 2015, Star Sports, Verizon Pro Kabaddi League
(d) 2014, Start Tv, Vivo Premier Kabaddi League

**2.2.** What is the ratio of the total number of viewers of the inaugural season vs. inaugural

championship?

(a) 5:1.5
(b) 5:1
(c) 1:5
(d) 5:4

**2.3.** Why was there a doubt that PKL would not be a success?

(a) There were many leagues attempting to emulate the IPL's business model and success
(b) There were fewer Kabaddi players known to the public
(c) Either (a) or (b)
(d) Both (a) and (b)

**2.4.** In what context is the word "zones" used in the passage?
(a) Disunions
(b) Divisions
(c) Directions
(d) Neighborhood

**2.5.** Because Kabaddi is played at grassroots community level, which kind of viewers it could

possibly attract?
(a) only rural viewers
(b) only urban views

(c) rural and metropolitan viewers
(d) it would garner no viewers at all

**2.6.** How many new teams in the fifth edition of the league were added?
(a) four
(b) two
(c) twenty
(d) five

**2.7.** Choose the word which is Most Similar to the word printed in bold in the passage:

**inception**
(a) initiation
(b) alternate
(c) closing
(d) none of the above

**2.8.** Choose the word which is Most Similar to the word printed in bold in the passage:

**era**
(a) gain
(b) formation
(c) time
(d) collection

**2.9.** Choose the word which is Most Opposite to the word printed in bold in the passage:

**emulate**
(a) create
(b) despise
(c) prepare
(d) share

**2.10.** Choose the word which is Most Opposite to the word printed in bold in the passage:

**intense**
(a) short
(b) dreadful
(c) mild
(d) none of the above

# PASSAGE-3

The great minds of the country had the ability to make others join their endeavor to convert dreams into reality. For them, the nation was bigger than themselves and they could draw thousands to act upon their dreams.

In December 2000, I had participated in the birth **centenary** celebrations of Adhyapaka Rathna T. Totadri Iyengar. I graduated in science from St. Joseph's College, Tiruchirapalli (1954). As a young student I saw Prof. T. Totadri Iyengar – a unique, divine–looking personality – walking through the college campus every morning and teaching mathematics to the students of B.Sc. (Honours) and M.Sc. The students looked at him with awe as one would at a guru, which indeed he was. When he walked, knowledge radiated all around. At that time, 'Calculus' Srinivasan was my mathematics teachers. He used to talk about Prof. Totadri Iyengar with deep respect and would organize integrated classes for first year B.Sc. (Honours) and first year B.Sc. (Physics) to be taught by him. I also had the opportunity to attend some of these classes, particularly on the subjects of modern algebra and statistics. When we were in first year B.Sc., 'Calculus' Srinivasan used to pick the top ten students as members of the Mathematics Club of St. Joseph's where Prof. Totadri Iyengar used to give a lecture series.

One day, in 1952, he gave a lecture on ancient mathematicians and astronomers of India. He spoke for nearly one hour. The lecture still rings in my ears. Let me share with you my thoughts about some **ancient** mathematicians, glimpses of whom I saw in Prof. Totadri Iyengar in my own way.

Aryabhata, born in 476 AD in Kusumapura (now called Patna), was an astronomer and mathematician. He was reputed to be a repository of all the mathematical knowledge known at that point of time. He was only twenty-three years old when he wrote *Aryabhatiyam* in two parts. The text covers arithmetic, algebra and trigonometry and, of course, astronomy. He gave formulae for the areas of a triangle and a circle and attempted to give the volumes of a sphere and a pyramid. He was the first to give an **approximation** to pi as the ratio of a circle's circumference and diameter, arriving at the value 3.1416. To celebrate this great astronomer, India named its first satellite launched in 1975 Aryabhata.

Brahmagupta was born in 598 AD at Billamala in Rajasthan in the empire of Harsha. He wrote the *Brahma Sphuta Siddhanta* at the age of thirty. He updated works of astronomy. He covered progressions and geometry. He also studied and gave what is known as the solution of **indeterminate** equations of different degrees as well as solutions to quadratic equations.

[**Source:** Ignited Minds: unleashing the power within India; Dr APJ Abdul Kalam; Pg. 40-43; Penguin Books Ltd.]

**3.1.** What were the great minds of the country capable of according to the passage?

    a.   to make others join their endeavor to convert dreams into reality
(b) to do nothing
(c) to make people play Kabaddi
(d) to make people opt for mathematics during their school days

**3.2.** Who is referred to as a unique, divine–looking personality in the passage?

(a) Dr. APJ Abdul Kalam
(b) Prof. T. Totadri Iyengar
(c) Aryabhata
(d) Prof. Srinivasan

**3.3.** Who is referred to as 'Calculus' in the given passage?

(a) Aryabhata
(b) Cannot say
(c) Srinivasan
(d) Not mentioned in the passage

**3.4.** To celebrate this great astronomer, India named its first __________ launched in 1975 Aryabhata?

(a) tank
(b) satellite
(c) car
(d) train

**3.5.** What all did Brahmagupta cover in the *Brahma Sphuta Siddhanta*?

(a) only geometry
(b) only trigonometry

(c) progressions and geometry
(d) none of the above

**3.6.** What is 'Kusumapura' now known as?

(a) Patna
(b) Gopalganj
(c) Chhapra
(d) Purnea

**3.7.** Choose the word which is Most Similar to the word printed in bold in the passage:

**centenary**
(a) 100th anniversary
(b) alternate
(c) closing
(d) none of the above

**3.8.** Choose the word which is Most Similar to the word printed in bold in the passage:

**ancient**
(a) fair
(b) bad

(c) primitive

(d) collection


**3.9.** Choose the word which is Most Opposite to the word printed in bold in the passage:

**approximation**

(a) creation

(b) variation

(c) preparation

(d) sharing


**3.10.** Choose the word which is Most Opposite to the word printed in bold in the passage:

**indeterminate**

(a) short

(b) dreadful

(c) definite

(d) vague

# PASSAGE-4

"1801— I have just returned from a visit to my landlord— the solitary neighbor that I shall be troubled with. This is certainly a beautiful country! In England, I do not believe that I could have fixed on a situation so completely removed from the stir of society. A perfect misanthropist's Heaven- and Mr. Heathcliff and I are such a suitable pair to divide the desolation between us. A capital fellow! He little imagined how my heart warmed towards him when I beheld his black eyes withdraw so suspiciously under their brows, as I rode up, and when his fingers sheltered themselves, with a jealous resolution, still further in his waistcoat, as I announced my name.

"Mr. Heathcliff?" I said.

A nod was the answer.

"Mr. Lockwood, your new tenant, sir—I do myself the honor of calling as soon as possible after my arrival, to express the hope that I have not inconvenienced you by my **perseverance** in soliciting the occupation of Thrushcross Grange. I heard, yesterday, you had had some thoughts—"

"Thrushcross Grange is my own sir," he interrupted, wincing, "I should not allow anyone to inconvenience me, if I could hinder it—walk in!"

The "walk in" was uttered with closed teeth and expressed the sentiment, "Go to the Deuce!" Even the gate over which he leant manifested no sympathizing movement to the words; and I think that circumstance determined me to accept the invitation: I felt interested in a man who seemed more exaggeratedly reserved than myself.

When he saw my horse's breast fairly pushing the **barrier**, he did pull out his hand to unchain it, and then sullenly preceded me up the causeway, as we entered the court:

"Joseph, take Mr. Lockwood's horse; and bring up some wine."

Joseph was an elderly, nay, an old man: very old, perhaps, though hale and sinewy.

"The Lord help us!" he soliloquized in an undertone of peevish displeasure, while relieving me of my horse: looking, meantime, in my face so sourly that I charitably conjectured he must have need of **divine** aid to digest his dinner, and his pious ejaculation had no reference to my unexpected advent.

Wuthering Heights is the name of Mr. Heathcliff's dwelling, "Wuthering" being significant provincial adjective, descriptive of the atmospheric tumult to which its station is exposed in stormy weather. Pure, bracing ventilation they must have up there, at all times, indeed: one may guess the power of the north wind, blowing over the edge, by the excessive slant of a few, stunted firs at the end of the house; and by a range of **gaunt** thorns all stretching their limbs one way, as if craving alms of the sun. That's it!"

[**Source:** Extracted and Edited from Wuthering Heights by Emily Bronte; Chapter-I; Page- 1&2]

**4.1.** Which year did the author return from a visit to his landlord?

(a) 1811
(b) 1801
(c) 1181
(d) none of the above

**4.2.** Who is the new tenant as given in the passage?

(a) Mr. Heathcliff
(b) Joseph
(c) Mr. Lockwood

(d) Thrushcross Grange


**4.3.** Who is referred to as 'a very old man, though, hale and sinewy' in the given passage?

(a) Joseph
(b) Deuce
(c) Mr. Lockwood
(d) Not mentioned in the passage


**4.4.** As per the passage, what does the word 'Wuthering' stand for?
(a) a horse's breast
(b) descriptive of the atmospheric tumult to which its station is exposed in stormy

weather
(c) a cart
(d) main character


**4.5.** According to the given passage, what/who is/are stretching their limbs one way, as if

craving alms of the sun?
(a) a range of gaunt thorns
(b) horse

(c) Joseph
(d) the clouds


**4.6.** What kind of a man is Mr. Heathcliff as per the passage?
(a) reserved
(b) jolly natured
(c) loud
(d) ever smiling

**4.7.** Choose the word which is Most Similar to the word printed in bold in the passage:

**perseverance**
(a) **patience**
(b) kind
(c) purity
(d) freedom


**4.8.** Choose the word which is Most Similar to the word printed in bold in the passage:
**barrier**
(a) fairly

(b) futuristic
(c) **hurdle**
(d) pressurize


**4.9.** Choose the word which is Most Opposite to the word printed in bold in the passage:
**divine**
(a) heavely
(b) godlike
(c) motherly
(d) **earthly**


**4.10.** Choose the word which is Most Opposite to the word printed in bold in the passage:
**gaunt**
(a) bony
(b) skeletal

(c) very thin
(d) **fat**

# PASSAGE-5

"This is Charles Dickens' true story:

'I am Born'

Whether I shall turn out to be the hero of my own life, or whether that station will be held by anybody else, these pages must show. To begin my life with the beginning of my life, I record that I was born on a Friday, at twelve o'clock at night. It was remarked that the clock began to strike, and I began to cry, **simultaneously**.

For the day and hour of my birth, it was declared by the nurse, and by some sage women in the neighborhood, first, that I was destined to be unlucky in life; and secondly, that I was privileged to see ghosts and spirits; both these gifts **inevitably** attaching, as they believed, to all unlucky infants of either gender, born towards the small hours on a Friday night.

I was born with a caul, which was advertised for sale, in the newspapers, at the low price of fifteen guineas. Whether sea–going people were short of money about that time, or were short of faith and preferred cork jackets, I don't know; all I know is, that there was but one solitary bidding, and that was from an attorney connected with the bill–broking business, who offered two pounds in cash, and the balance in sherry, but declined to be guaranteed from drowning on any higher bargain. And ten years afterwards, the caul was put up in a raffle down in our part of the country, to fifty members at half–a–crown a head, the winner to spend five shillings. I was present myself, and I remember to have felt quite uncomfortable and confused, at a part of myself being disposed of in that way. The caul was won, by an old lady with a hand–basket, who, very reluctantly, produced from it the stipulated five shillings, all in halfpence, and two pence half penny short. It is a fact which will be long remembered as remarkable down there, that she was never drowned, but died triumphantly in bed, at ninety–two. I have understood that it was, to the last, her proudest boast, that she never had been on the water in her life, except upon a bridge; and that over her tea (to which she was extremely partial) she, to the last, expressed her **indignation** at the impiety of mariners and others, who had the presumption to go 'meandering' about the world. It was in vain to represent to her that some conveniences, tea perhaps included, resulted from this objectionable practice. She always returned, with greater emphasis and with an **instinctive** knowledge of the strength of her objection, 'Let us have no meandering.'"

[**Source:** Extracted, with edits and revisions, from *David Copperfield* by Charles Dickens]

**5.1.**How is the tone of the passage?

(a) pensive

(b) comic

(c) depressing

(d) earnest

**5.2.** When was the author born?

(a) 10 o'clock on a Friday

(b) 12 o' clock on a Friday

(c) 11 o'clock on a Friday

(d) midnight 12 o'clock on a Friday

**5.3.** Which 'objectionable practice' does the writer refer to by "*It was in vain to represent to her that some conveniences, tea perhaps included, resulted from this objectionable practice?*"

(a) never going on the water

(b) the water in tea

(c) the trips of the sailors

(d) the visits upon the bridge

**5.4.** How many times was the caul auctioned?

(a) once

(b) twice

(c) thrice

(d) none of the above

**5.5.** What does the word 'reluctantly' mean according to the passage?

(a) warmly

(b) favourably

(c) unwillingly

(d) carefully

**5.6.** Most probably, the chapter seems to be-

(a) an excerpt of a story of the writer's caul auction

(b) an excerpt from the last chapter of a book

(c) an excerpt from the first chapter of a book

(d) a chapter of a book on natural science and related myths

**5.7.** Choose the word which is Most Similar to the word printed in bold in the passage:

**simultaneously**
(a) 100<sup>th</sup> anniversary

(b) alternate
(c) closing
(d) none of the above

**5.8.** Choose the word which is Most Similar to the word printed in bold in the passage:

**inevitably**

(a) fair
(b) bad
(c) primitive
(d) collection

**5.9.** Choose the word which is Most Opposite to the word printed in bold in the passage:

**indignation**

(a) creation
(b) variation
(c) preparation
(d) sharing

**5.10.** Choose the word which is Most Opposite to the word printed in bold in the passage:

**instinctive**

(a) short
(b) dreadful
(c) definite
(d) vague

# PASSAGE-6

Dear Ashutosh,

Hope you are doing well!

I read your e-mail and got to know about your concern for improving your command on English language. I wish to express that if you'd like to improve your English, one thing you can do is to build up your vocabulary. In order to do this, you have to practice a lot. I'm afraid there is not a short cut for this. But there are many effective ways. First of all, you should read a lot. You can read short stories, comics, newspapers, magazines etc. depending on your English level. As you read, you can try to guess the meanings of unknown words from the context of the sentence. If you cannot, then look up the definition in a dictionary. English to English dictionary should be your first choice and keep the **translator** as last. Another way of building **vocabulary** is to watch movies in English which will also help with pronunciation. Try to be involved with the language as much as you can. Maintain a vocabulary notebook and write down a few words each day. Keep in mind that you have to revise them regularly. In my opinion, to communicate with people all you need is words. Even if you just say the words one after another, people most likely will understand what you mean regardless of the order of the words and grammatical construction.

Bye for now. Take care and try to practice the above mentioned suggestions in order to get positive results.

Dear Prakriti,

I'm better now. Thanks!

It's been a month I haven't heard from you. I hope you are well. Thanks for suggesting ways to improve my command on the language. I will surely try to work upon the suggestions given by you.

I must tell you, Prakriti that I had a **terrible** day at school yesterday. My friends and I were playing football in the school yard when I suddenly fell and twisted my ankle. At first I didn't experience much pain, but shortly it started hurting badly. I had difficulty walking so my friends helped me around. They took me to a hospital and stayed with me until my parents arrived. The doctor said it was broken and I needed to rest for a month. We came home last night and I feel better now. This unpleasant incident also made me realize how **valuable** friendships are. One needs a true friend for sure to be able to stay calm and get good advice. I don't know what I would do without them. So I want to say I feel happy to have excellent friends like you.

Do take good care of yourself and keep writing.



**6.1.** What is the objective of the e-mail drafted by Prakriti?

    a.  Difficulties of learning English
(b) Problems of learning a second language alone
(c) What's the best way of learning English
(d) What can we do to improve our English

**6.2.** According to the first e-mail, which of the following is incorrect?

(a) We should read a lot
(b) We should take notes when we learn new words
(c) We should use a translator for all the unknown words

(d) We should practice as much as we can


**6.3.** What is the most important thing to communicate with people according to the writer?

(a) Grammar
(b) Vocabulary
(c) Order of the words used
(d) Advanced English course


**6.4.** Is watching English movies helpful in improving one's vocabulary in the language?
(a) Not at all
(b) Yes
(c) Not known

(d) Can't say


**6.5.** Which of the following is incorrect, according to the second e-mail?
(a) Ashutosh injured his ankle

(b) Ashutosh's friends helped him get to a hospital
(c) Ashutosh hurt his arm
(d) Ashutosh won't be able to go to school for a month


**6.6.** According to the second e-mail, what does Ashutosh want to emphasize in his e-mail?
(a) He should stop playing volleyball
(b) The terrible day he had
(c) The importance of school
(d) The importance of friendship

**6.7.** Choose the word which is Most Similar to the word printed in bold in the passage
**translator**
(a) interpreter
(b) dignitary
(c) manager
(d) none of the above


**6.8.** Choose the word which is Most Similar to the word printed in bold in the passage.

**vocabulary**
(a) language
(b) lexicon
(c) letters
(d) alphabet


**6.9.** Choose the word which is Most Opposite to the word printed in bold in the passage.
**terrible**
(a) dingy
(b) opposite
(c) slight
(d) flawless


**6.10.** Choose the word which is Most Opposite to the word printed in bold in the passage.
**valuable**
(a) worthless
(b) hearty
(c) mighty
(d) righteous

No society can ever function smoothly without having a structured system. By civil society is meant an entire array of organized groups and institutions that are independent of the state, voluntary, and at least to some extent self generating and self reliant. This encompasses non-governmental organizations, independent mass media, think tanks, universities, and social and religious groups. Civil society contributes to good governance by being an overseer- against human rights infringement and governance deficit, voice of the weaker sections' point of view, an agitated voice of aggrieved citizens, service provider to areas and people not reached by efforts by the officials, etc. Civil society groups may establish ties to political parties and the state, but they have got to hold on to their independence, and they do not **look for** political power for themselves.

As far as the Democratic societies are concerned, they, from the earliest times, have expected their governments to protect the weak against the strong. No 'era of good feeling' can justify discharging the police force or giving up the idea of public control over concentrated private wealth. Conversely speaking, it is evident that a spirit of self-denial and moderation on the part of those who hold economic power will significantly mitigate the demand for utter impartiality. Men are extra concerned about liberty and security than in an equal distribution of wealth. The extent to which Government must hinder with business, consequently, is not exactly measured by the extent to which economic power is concentrated into a few hands.

The **mandatory** degree of government intervention depends chiefly on whether economic powers are oppressively used, and on the inevitability of keeping economic factors in a bearable state of steadiness. But with the necessity of meeting all these dangers and threats to liberty, the powers of government are unavoidably augmented, whichever political party may be in office. The expansion of government is an obvious outcome of the growth of technology and of the problems that go with the use of machines and science. Since the government in our nation, must take on more powers to meet its problems, there is no way to conserve freedom other than by making democracy further potently dominant.

**7.1.** The advent of science and technology has increased the

    a.   tyranny of the political parties
    b.   chances of economic inequality
    c.   powers of the government
    d.   freedom of people

**7.2** Which of the following is NOT TRUE in the context of the passage?

    a.   civil society contributes to good governance
    b.   civil society is an entire array of organized groups and institutions that are

independent of the state

    a.   civil society groups would never establish ties to political parties and the state
    b.   all of the above

**7.3.** A spirit of moderation on the economically sound people would make the less privileged

    a.  unhappy with their lot
    b.  clamor less for absolute equality
    c.  more interested in freedom and security
    d.  unhappy with the affluent class

**7.4.** The growth of government is necessitated to

    a.  make the rich and the poor happy
    b.  curb the accumulation of wealth in a few hands
    c.  monitor science and technology
    d.  deploy the police force wisely

**7.5.** 'Era of good feeling' in second paragraph refers to

    a.  time without government
    b.  time of adversity
    c.  time of prosperity
    d.  time of police atrocities

**7.6.** 'Bearable state of steadiness' in the last paragraph may indicate

    a.  an adequate number of police force
    b.  a reasonable level of economic equality
    c.  a reasonable check on economic power
    d.  a reasonable amount of government interference

**7.7.** According to the passage, what do democratic societies expect of their government?

    a.  to do nothing
    b.  to maintain an autocratic rule
    c.  to protect the weak against the strong
    d.  to be quiet

**7.8.** Which of the following is what man is extra concerned about, according to the above passage?

    a.  conscience
    b.  demand and supply
    c.  political gains
    d.  liberty and security

**7.9.** Which of the following is the meaning of the phrase look for as used in the passage?

    a.  to search

b.  leave

c.  discuss

d.  protest

**7.10.** Give the synonym of the word **mandatory** as used in the passage

a.  goodness

b.  extraordinary

c.  able

d.  obligatory

# PASSAGE-8

As is rightly said that, *An ounce of patience is worth a pound of brains* which lays prominence on the fact that persistence is far better than intelligence, by and large. Although, we do know that it's easily said than done as most of us fail to follow it the way we laud it.

In the current testing times of the Covid 19 situation, we see the significance of having endurance when we have no power over the circumstances. Nevertheless, having patience and controlling our feelings may do wonders as far as overcoming any such given depressing state of affairs are concerned. It depends completely on our mind-set as to whether we choose to whimper and complain or to wait for the right time patiently and remain calm and composed until the things get better.

Patience in this hour is the key apart from taking care of each other, helping the needy, doing our parts in fighting the virus by staying indoors and adhering to the covid appropriate behavioural norms.

The government bodies have a challenging job to keep us and this country safe. Let us not make their job more difficult by flouting the rules and containment measures.

As a matter of fact, one should always keep in mind the adage- *this too shall pass*! Therefore, instead of thinking that it's only me who is in distress and all others are having a gala time. One should, rather, understand that things are similar with others too; though, these could be at different point in time, in case of others. Consequently, it could be concluded that things would become simple if one merely accepts life and its challenges as they come. We shall, surely, defeat this crisis. Eventually, we will crush this viciously invisible enemy, and, are sure to beat it with a spirit of camaraderie and kindness to keep this nation protected and strong.

**8.1.** Which of the below most suitably explains the comment *an ounce of patience is worth a*

*pound of brains*:

    a.  Patience comes first, intelligence next
    b.  All the people are wise
    c.  Patience is of no use
    d.  Without patience, it's impossible to use intelligence completely

**8.2.** What does the following phrase imply- people consider other person's problems to be light and their own life full of obstacles and issues?

    a.  They are self-centered
    b.  They are baffled
    c.  They get worried and sad
    d.  They feel that they alone face serious problems while others have a pleasant time

**8.3.** Which of the following statements is TRUE according to the given passage?

a. Wisdom is of no use
b. Patience is mediocre
c. Patience is far better than wisdom
d. None of the above

**8.4.** Which of the following may do wonders as far as overcoming any given off-putting circumstances are concerned?

a. Scientific inventions
b. Patience and controlling our thoughts
c. Riches and authority
d. One's destiny

**8.5.** Which of the following is the most appropriate title for the given passage?

a. This too shall pass
b. Patience is pretty hard to follow
c. Busy people are tolerant
d. Complicatedness and its solutions

# PASSAGE-9

The Dalai Lama's 86th birthday, celebrated on Tuesday, made headlines here for an unusual reason – PM Modi had greeted the Tibetan spiritual leader. The public acknowledgement is, of course, a subtle recalibration in the China policy as he's persona non grata for China. However, it also shows the limited number of cards India has as it confronts a belligerent China.

China recently celebrated the centenary of the Communist Party of China (CPC). India's challenge was amplified in the speech delivered by Xi Jinping. Its tenor signalled a China that will be even more confrontational. It poses a tricky challenge. Especially since commanders from the two militaries are scheduled to meet, for the 12th time, to work out a disengagement from friction points on the LAC in eastern Ladakh.

After China's unilateral ingress last year, in violation of existing border agreements, India negotiated disengagement this year at one friction point – Pangong Tso. However, there has been no progress on disengagement in Demchok, Gogra, Hot Springs and Depsang. China's actions and their scale have altered the bilateral relationship. GoI has begun to scale back the economic engagement. Noticeably, in keeping China out of the forthcoming 5G transition and parts of the tech market.

An important takeaway for India is that the size and the sophistication of the domestic economy matters in securing strategic interests. China's increasing belligerence has accompanied its growing economic clout that is backed by a $14.7 trillion GDP. As India works on its economic transformation, it should deepen its ties with Taiwan, a global leader in semiconductors. Deepening ties will simultaneously serve India's economic interests and send China a message. Being deferential to China's sensitivities won't help India's cause.

[**Source:** Confronting Xi: India should engage both the Dalai Lama and Taiwan July 7, 2021, 10:29 PM IST TOI Edit in TOI Editorials, India. https://timesofindia.indiatimes.com/blogs/toi-editorials/confronting-xi-india-should-engage-both-the-dalai-lama-and-taiwan/]

**9.1.** According to the passage what does the following statement mean- 'persona non grata'?

a) An unacceptable or unwelcome person

b) Mentally unfit person

c) Selfless person

d) An old person

**9.2.** What did China recently celebrate?

a) Nothing

b) Not known

c) The centenary of the Communist Party of China

d) Dalai Lama's 86th birthday

**9.3.** What does the expression bottleneck refer to as used in the passage?

a) Christianity

b) Journalism

c) People using bottles

d) Is a situation that stops a process or activity from progressing

**9.4.** Which of the following statements as given in the above passage is TRUE?

a) All Refugees are inhuman

b) The Refugees need to be deserted

c) The Refugees deserve a new lease on life

d) We should neither be compassionate nor empathize with anybody

**9.5.** Which of the following words is the most OPPOSITE in meaning to decree as used in the passage?

a) Request

b) Rare

c) Experiment

d) Cancellation

# PASSAGE-10

I recently had to sign a big card - which is a horror unto itself, especially as the keeper of the Big Card was leaning over me at the time. Suddenly I was on the spot, a rabbit in the headlights, torn between doing a fun message or some sort of in-joke or a drawing. Instead overwhelmed by the innumerable options on hand, I decided to just write: "Good luck, best, Joe!"

To my shock, the next I found out that I had forgotten how to put my thoughts in writing. My entire way of life is "tap letters into computer". Even my shopping lists are hidden in the notes function of my phone. If I have to memorise something I immediately shoot an e-mail to myself. While under pressure to think, I chew a pen for better concentration. Paper is something I stack under my laptop to make it a more hassle-free height for me to type on with an ease.

Bic found by conducting an opinion poll of 1,000 teens by the stationers, that one in 10 don't possess a pen, a third have never written a letter, and half of 13 to 19 years old have never been forced to sit down and jot down even a thank you letter. More than 80% have never written a love letter, 56% don't have letter paper at home. And a quarter has never experienced the matchless agony of writing a birthday card. If at all a teen ever has used a pen is mainly on an exam paper.

Bic needs to recognize the changing priorities of the teens. Have you heard of smart phones, e-mail, face book and snap chatting? This is the future. Pens and Paper cease to exist. Handwriting is a relic.

"Handwriting is one of the most creative outlets we have and should be given the same importance as other art forms such as sketching, painting or photography."

[**Source:** Extracted, with edits and revisions, from https://www.jagranjosh.com/articles/ugc-net-reading-comprehension-questions-with-answers-1560863903-1]

**10.1. When confronted with signing a big card, the author felt like "a rabbit in the headlight"**

**(first paragraph). What does this phrase mean?**

    a.   a state of confusion
    b.   a state of pleasure
    c.   a state of anxiety
    d.   a state of pain

**10.2. According to the author, which one is NOT the most creative outlet of pursuit?**

    a.   Photography
    b.   Handwriting
    c.   Sketching
    d.   reading

**10.3.** The primary purpose of the passage is most likely to

    a.   express significance of writing

b.   clarify the motivation behind an artist's work

c.   contrast sketching and photography

d.   getting confused while typing

**10.4. The entire existence of the author revolves round:**

a.   computer

b.   mobile phone

c.   typewriter

d.   both (a) and (b)

**10.5. How many teens, as per the Bic survey, do not own a pen?**

a.   800

b.   500

c.   130

d.   100

**10.6. What is the main concern of the author?**

a.   that the teens use social networks for communication

b.   that the teens use mobile phones

c.   that the teens use computer

d.   that the teens have forgotten the art of handwriting

**10.7.** Which of the following is NOT TRUE as per the second paragraph?

a.   that the author writes extensively

b.   that the author uses mobile even for making a shopping list

c.   that the author places a heap of papers under his laptop

d.   that the author doesn't enjoy writing

**10.8.** Choose the word which is most similar in meaning to **innumerable** as used in the

passage.

a.   similar

b.   multifarious

c.   descending

d.   social

**10.9.** Choose the word which is most opposite in meaning to the word outlet as used in the last paragraph
of the given passage.

a.   despair

b.  narrow

   c.  out

d.  ingress

**10.10.How many teens, as per the Bic survey, have never written a love letter?**

a.   100 per cent

b.   1 per cent

c.   More than 80 per cent

d.   Less than 80 per cent

# ANSWER KEY TO THE PASSAGES [ENGLISH LANGUAGE]

# PASSAGE-1

Elections were in the air of the world's youngest democracy when I arrived in Thimphu. This was for a by-election in the capital city that dominated the conversation at dinners, even in Thimphu's most fun night-spot Mojo Park (the best music in town). Bhutan has taken to democracy with ease ever since 2008 when the first proper elections were held, a process India has helped out with, sending officials from the Election Commission travelling to check arrangements, explain electronic voting machine (EVM) technology and procedures.

Monks and nuns in this deeply religious Buddhist majority are not allowed to vote, so as to avoid mixing religion and politics. All voters must wear their national dress on polling day, but no one—candidate, campaigner or voter—is allowed to wear the kabney silk and gyentag (scarf of honour, for men and women respectively, bestowed only by the King), patang (ceremonial sword), or any other sign of rank or royal patronage to avoid a misuse of influence.

In Thimphu, the Textile Museum is run by the Royal Textile Academy - project of Ashi Sangay Choden Wangchuck, one of the Queen Mothers of Bhutan (the former King had four Queens, all sisters). The museum is dedicated to preserving the oldest and rarest woven fabrics worn in Bhutan and used in their religious **scrolls** and Thangkhas. As you walk in, it is the 'Thongdrel' or massive silk work of the Zhabdrung Phuensum Tshogpa (in honour of a sacred meal served to Bhutan's political and spiritual founder in 1637) that greets you. The thongdrel stands 34 feet tall, running 23 feet across and is set against a glass window that runs three stories high.

Tara Lakhang and Pangrizampa monastery on the **outskirts** of Thimphu is Bhutan's only monastery dedicated to 21 Taras, the female Bodhisattva and it is a powerful display of ancient feminism.

While polygamy is practiced in some parts, so is polyandry, and divorce settlements are equal and even-handed. Even so, Bhutanese women lag behind in one place that it counts: parliament. In the last National Assembly elections, 3/4ths of the 47 seats had only male candidates (nine had females), and four women were elected as MPs. "**Misogyny** plays only one part of it," explains the only leader of a party (DCT) Lily Wangchuk, who runs a hotel in downtown Thimphu. "Women just don't vote for women, and the lack of women role models in modern

Bhutan becomes a vicious cycle."

The Kyichu Lhakhang, in Paro, is one of Bhutan's oldest and simplest monasteries, believed to be constructed in 659 CE, by Tibetan king Songtsen Gampo.

All year round, one is welcomed into Kyichu with a spectacular and miraculous orange tree **laden** with fruit.

[**Source:** Extracted and Edited from The Hindu; APRIL 01, 2017)

**1.1.** Which of the following statements is/are correct regarding the 2008 Elections of Bhutan?

    I.  India helped Bhutan in elections by sending officials from Election Commission of India.

I. Monks and nuns were not allowed to vote.
II. Wearing National Dress on Election Day was compulsory.

a. I and II only
(b) II and III only
(c) I and III only
(d) **All are Correct**

**1.2.** Who is 'Ashi Sangay Choden Wangchuck' as mentioned in the passage?

(a) The elected Prime Minister of Bhutan
(b) The elected President of Bhutan
(c) **Queen Mother of Bhutan**
(d) None is Correct

**1.3.** Consider the following statements regarding the 'Mojo Park' as mentioned in the passage.

I. It is situated in the Northeast India
II. It is famous for its Music Shows
III. It is situated in the City of Thimphu

(a) All are Correct
(b) **II and III only**
(c) I and III only
(d) I and II only

**1.4.** Which of the following statements is correct as given in the Passage?
(a) Polyandry is not practiced in Bhutan
(b) **Polygamy is practiced in Bhutan**
(c) There is not a single Female Member in Bhutan's Parliament
(d) None is Correct

**1.5.** Why was candidate, campaigner or voter not allowed to wear any sign of rank or royal patronage in the 2008 Elections of the country?

(a) Due to some kind of superstition.
(b) Due to some kind of superstition.
(c) **To neglect the misuse of influence of wealthy and famous people**
(d) None is Correct

**1.6.** Consider the following statements regarding the 'Kyichu Lhakhang' as given in the passage:

I. He was the first Prime Minister of Bhutan.

II. It is one of Bhutan's oldest monasteries.

III. It was built in 7<sup>th</sup> Century.

(a) I and II only

(b) **II and III only**

(c) I and III only

(d) None is Correct

**1.7.** Choose the word which is Most Similar to the word printed in bold in the passage

**Scrolls**

(a) **Document**

(b) Aimless

(c) Rolling

(d) None is Correct

**1.8.** Choose the word which is Most Similar to the word printed in bold in the passage.

**Outskirts**

(a) **Periphery**

(b) Center

(c) Downtown

(d) Away

**1.9.** Choose the word which is Most Opposite to the word printed in bold in the passage.

**Laden**

(a) **Empty**

(b) Full

(c) Charged

(d) Encumbered

**1.10.** Choose the word which is Most Opposite to the word printed in bold in the passage.

**Misogyny**

(a) Woman-hater

(b) Sexist

(c) **Feminist**

(d) None is Correct

# PASSAGE-2

Kabaddi has been one of the most underrated sports for long. Vivo Pro Kabaddi is a ground-breaking initiative by Mashal Sports Pvt. Ltd and Star India Pvt. Ltd. Ever since its **inception** in 2014, the League has revolutionised the sport of Kabaddi with stunning innovations, making it an inspirational sport for players and fans alike.

The league's inception was influenced by the popularity of the Kabaddi tournament at the 2006 Asian Games. The format of the competition was influenced by Indian Premier League. The Pro Kabaddi League uses a franchise-based model and its first season was held in 2014 with eight teams each of which having paid fees of up to US$250,000 to join.

Mashal Sports and STAR India have jointly worked towards elevating the sport of Kabaddi to an international standard with new and exciting innovations in the rules and how the game is viewed, thus heralding in a new **era** for Kabaddi. They infused new life into the sport by bringing it to the major metropolitan cities of India along with regions where Kabaddi was yet to gain a foothold. Vivo Pro Kabaddi now has unprecedented participation from various parts of the country owing to the outreach over the past seasons and the advent of new programmes pioneered by Mashal Sports to encourage young talent from across the country. Kabaddi is now also seen as a viable career option by various aspiring players in India and abroad.

There were doubts over whether the PKL would be successful, noting that there were many leagues attempting to **emulate** the IPL's business model and success, and that unlike cricket, there were relatively fewer well-known players in Kabaddi. However, it was also noted that Kabaddi was widely played in grassroots community settings, and could thus attract a wide variety of rural and metropolitan viewers for advertisers to target if the league gained significant traction.

The addition of four new teams in the fifth edition of the league made vivo Pro Kabaddi India's biggest sports league in terms of geographical representation and number of teams. The new sides – Gujarat Fortunegiants, Haryana Steelers, Tamil Thalaivas and U.P. Yoddha made the competition all the more **intense** and the Kabaddi all the more exciting.

The inaugural season was seen by 435 million viewers, Mashal sports placing it just behind the total-season viewership of the 2014 Indian Premier League season, while the inaugural championship was seen by 86.4 million viewers. Star Sports, the PKL's broadcaster, subsequently announced in 2015 that it would acquire a 74% stake in the league's parent company Mashal Sports.

For the 2017 season, the PKL added four new teams, and changed its format to split the teams into two divisions known as "zones".

[**Source:** Extracted and Edited from https://www.mbarendezvous.com/easy-reading-comprehension-passages/]

**2.1.** When was the professional Kabaddi league (PKL) started, who was the broadcast partner

and what is it currently called?

a.   **2014, Start Sports, Vivo Pro Kabaddi League**
(b) 2014, Zee Tv, Verizon Premier Kabaddi League
(c) 2015, Star Sports, Verizon Pro Kabaddi League
(d) 2014, Start Tv, Vivo Premier Kabaddi League

**2.2.** What is the ratio of the total number of viewers of the inaugural season vs. inaugural

championship?

(a) 5:1.5
(b) **5:1**
(c) 1:5
(d) 5:4

**2.3.** Why was there a doubt that PKL would not be a success?

(a) There were many leagues attempting to emulate the IPL's business model and success
(b) There were fewer Kabaddi players known to the public
(c) Either (a) or (b)
(d) **Both (a) and (b)**

**2.4.** In what context is the word "zones" used in the passage?
(a) Disunions
(b) **Divisions**
(c) Directions
(d) Neighborhood

**2.5.** Because Kabaddi is played at grassroots community level, which kind of viewers it could

possibly attract?
(a) only rural viewers
(b) only urban views

(c) **rural and metropolitan viewers**
(d) it would garner no viewers at all

**2.6.** How many new teams in the fifth edition of the league were added?
(a) **four**
(b) two
(c) twenty
(d) five

**2.7.** Choose the word which is Most Similar to the word printed in bold in the passage:

**inception**
(a) **initiation**
(b) alternate
(c) closing
(d) none of the above


**2.8.** Choose the word which is Most Similar to the word printed in bold in the passage:
**era**
(a) gain
(b) formation
(c) **time**
(d) collection


**2.9.** Choose the word which is Most Opposite to the word printed in bold in the passage:
**emulate**
(a) create
(b) **despise**
(c) prepare
(d) share


**2.10.** Choose the word which is Most Opposite to the word printed in bold in the passage:
**intense**
(a) short
(b) dreadful
(c) **mild**
(d) none of the above

# PASSAGE-3

The great minds of the country had the ability to make others join their endeavor to convert dreams into reality. For them, the nation was bigger than themselves and they could draw thousands to act upon their dreams.

In December 2000, I had participated in the birth **centenary** celebrations of Adhyapaka Rathna T. Totadri Iyengar. I graduated in science from St. Joseph's College, Tiruchirapalli (1954). As a young student I saw Prof. T. Totadri Iyengar – a unique, divine–looking personality – walking through the college campus every morning and teaching mathematics to the students of B.Sc. (Honours) and M.Sc. The students looked at him with awe as one would at a guru, which indeed he was. When he walked, knowledge radiated all around. At that time, 'Calculus' Srinivasan was my mathematics teachers. He used to talk about Prof. Totadri Iyengar with deep respect and would organize integrated classes for first year B.Sc. (Honours) and first year B.Sc. (Physics) to be taught by him. I also had the opportunity to attend some of these classes, particularly on the subjects of modern algebra and statistics. When we were in first year B.Sc., 'Calculus' Srinivasan used to pick the top ten students as members of the Mathematics Club of St. Joseph's where Prof. Totadri Iyengar used to give a lecture series.

One day, in 1952, he gave a lecture on ancient mathematicians and astronomers of India. He spoke for nearly one hour. The lecture still rings in my ears. Let me share with you my thoughts about some **ancient** mathematicians, glimpses of whom I saw in Prof. Totadri Iyengar in my own way.

Aryabhata, born in 476 AD in Kusumapura (now called Patna), was an astronomer and mathematician. He was reputed to be a repository of all the mathematical knowledge known at that point of time. He was only twenty-three years old when he wrote *Aryabhatiyam* in two parts. The text covers arithmetic, algebra and trigonometry and, of course, astronomy. He gave formulae for the areas of a triangle and a circle and attempted to give the volumes of a sphere and a pyramid. He was the first to give an **approximation** to pi as the ratio of a circle's circumference and diameter, arriving at the value 3.1416. To celebrate this great astronomer, India named its first satellite launched in 1975 Aryabhata.

Brahmagupta was born in 598 AD at Billamala in Rajasthan in the empire of Harsha. He wrote the *Brahma Sphuta Siddhanta* at the age of thirty. He updated works of astronomy. He covered progressions and geometry. He also studied and gave what is known as the solution of **indeterminate** equations of different degrees as well as solutions to quadratic equations.

[**Source:** Ignited Minds: unleashing the power within India; Dr APJ Abdul Kalam; Pg. 40-43; Penguin Books Ltd.]

**3.1.** What were the great minds of the country capable of according to the passage?

(a)**to make others join their endeavor to convert dreams into reality**
(b) to do nothing
(c) to make people play Kabaddi
(d) to make people opt for mathematics during their school days

**3.2.** Who is referred to as a unique, divine–looking personality in the passage?

(a) Dr. APJ Abdul Kalam
(b) **Prof. T. Totadri Iyengar**
(c) Aryabhata
(d) Prof. Srinivasan


**3.3.** Who is referred to as 'Calculus' in the given passage?

(a) Aryabhata
(b) Cannot say
(c) **Srinivasan**
(d) Not mentioned in the passage


**3.4.** To celebrate this great astronomer, India named its first __________ launched in 1975 Aryabhata?
(a) tank
(b) **satellite**
(c) car
(d) train


**3.5.** What all did Brahmagupta cover in the *Brahma Sphuta Siddhanta*?
(a) only geometry
(b) only trigonometry

(c) **progressions and geometry**
(d) none of the above


**3.6.** What is 'Kusumapura' now known as?
(a) **Patna**
(b) Gopalganj
(c) Chhapra
(d) Purnea

**3.7.** Choose the word which is Most Similar to the word printed in bold in the passage:

centenary
(a) **100<sup>th</sup> anniversary**
(b) alternate
(c) closing
(d) none of the above


**3.8.** Choose the word which is Most Similar to the word printed in bold in the passage:
ancient
(a) fair
(b) bad

(c) **primitive**

(d) collection


**3.9.** Choose the word which is Most Opposite to the word printed in bold in the passage:

**approximation**

(a) creation

(b) **variation**

(c) preparation

(d) sharing


**3.10.** Choose the word which is Most Opposite to the word printed in bold in the passage:

**indeterminate**

(a) short

(b) dreadful

(c) **definite**

(d) vague

# PASSAGE-4

"1801— I have just returned from a visit to my landlord— the solitary neighbor that I shall be troubled with. This is certainly a beautiful country! In England, I do not believe that I could have fixed on a situation so completely removed from the stir of society. A perfect misanthropist's Heaven- and Mr. Heathcliff and I are such a suitable pair to divide the desolation between us. A capital fellow! He little imagined how my heart warmed towards him when I beheld his black eyes withdraw so suspiciously under their brows, as I rode up, and when his fingers sheltered themselves, with a jealous resolution, still further in his waistcoat, as I announced my name.

"Mr. Heathcliff?! I said.

A nod was the answer.

"Mr. Lockwood, your new tenant, sir—I do myself the honor of calling as soon as possible after my arrival, to express the hope that I have not inconvenienced you by my **perseverance** in soliciting the occupation of Thrushcross Grange. I heard, yesterday, you had had some thoughts—"

"Thrushcross Grange is my own sir," he interrupted, wincing, "I should not allow anyone to inconvenience me, if I could hinder it—walk in!"

The "walk in" was uttered with closed teeth and expressed the sentiment, "Go to the Deuce!" Even the gate over which he leant manifested no sympathizing movement to the words; and I think that circumstance determined me to accept the invitation: I felt interested in a man who seemed more exaggeratedly reserved than myself.

When he saw my horse's breast fairly pushing the **barrier**, he did pull out his hand to unchain it, and then sullenly preceded me up the causeway, as we entered the court:

"Joseph, take Mr. Lockwood's horse; and bring up some wine."

Joseph was an elderly, nay, an old man: very old, perhaps, though hale and sinewy.

"The Lord help us!" he soliloquized in an undertone of peevish displeasure, while relieving me of my horse: looking, meantime, in my face so sourly that I charitably conjectured he must have need of **divine** aid to digest his dinner, and his pious ejaculation had no reference to my unexpected advent.

Wuthering Heights is the name of Mr. Heathcliff's dwelling, "Wuthering" being significant provincial adjective, descriptive of the atmospheric tumult to which its station is exposed in stormy weather. Pure, bracing ventilation they must have up there, at all times, indeed: one may guess the power of the north wind, blowing over the edge, by the excessive slant of a few, stunted firs at the end of the house; and by a range of **gaunt** thorns all stretching their limbs one way, as if craving alms of the sun. That's it!"

[**Source:** Extracted and Edited from Wuthering Heights by Emily Bronte; Chapter-I; Page- 1&2]

**4.1.** Which year did the author return from a visit to his landlord?

(a) 1811
(b) **1801**
(c) 1181
(d) none of the above

**4.2.** Who is the new tenant as given in the passage?

(a) Mr. Heathcliff
(b) Joseph
(c) **Mr. Lockwood**

(d) Thrushcross Grange

**4.3.** Who is referred to as 'a very old man, though, hale and sinewy' in the given passage?

(a) **Joseph**
(b) Deuce
(c) Mr. Lockwood
(d) Not mentioned in the passage

**4.4.** As per the passage, what does the word 'Wuthering' stand for?
(a) a horse's breast
(b) **descriptive of the atmospheric tumult to which its station is exposed in stormy weather**
(c) a cart
(d) main character

**4.5.** According to the given passage, what/who is/are stretching their limbs one way, as if

craving alms of the sun?
(a) **a range of gaunt thorns**
(b) horse

(c) Joseph
(d) the clouds

**4.6.** What kind of a man is Mr. Heathcliff as per the passage?
(a) **reserved**
(b) jolly natured
(c) loud
(d) ever smiling

**4.7.** Choose the word which is Most Similar to the word printed in bold in the passage:

**perseverance**
(a) **patience**

(b) kind
(c) purity
(d) freedom

**4.8.** Choose the word which is Most Similar to the word printed in bold in the passage:
**barrier**
(a) fairly

(b) futuristic
(c) **hurdle**
(d) pressurize

**4.9.** Choose the word which is Most Opposite to the word printed in bold in the passage:
**divine**
(a) heavely
(b) godlike
(c) motherly
(d) **earthly**

**4.10.** Choose the word which is Most Opposite to the word printed in bold in the passage:
**gaunt**
(a) bony
(b) skeletal

(c) very thin
(d) **fat**

# PASSAGE-5

"This is Charles Dickens' true story:

'I am Born'

Whether I shall turn out to be the hero of my own life, or whether that station will be held by anybody else, these pages must show. To begin my life with the beginning of my life, I record that I was born on a Friday, at twelve o'clock at night. It was remarked that the clock began to strike, and I began to cry, **simultaneously**.

For the day and hour of my birth, it was declared by the nurse, and by some sage women in the neighborhood, first, that I was destined to be unlucky in life; and secondly, that I was privileged to see ghosts and spirits; both these gifts **inevitably** attaching, as they believed, to all unlucky infants of either gender, born towards the small hours on a Friday night.

I was born with a caul, which was advertised for sale, in the newspapers, at the low price of fifteen guineas. Whether sea–going people were short of money about that time, or were short of faith and preferred cork jackets, I don't know; all I know is, that there was but one solitary bidding, and that was from an attorney connected with the bill–broking business, who offered two pounds in cash, and the balance in sherry, but declined to be guaranteed from drowning on any higher bargain. And ten years afterwards, the caul was put up in a raffle down in our part of the country, to fifty members at half–a–crown a head, the winner to spend five shillings. I was present myself, and I remember to have felt quite uncomfortable and confused, at a part of myself being disposed of in that way. The caul was won, by an old lady with a hand–basket, who, very reluctantly, produced from it the stipulated five shillings, all in halfpence, and two pence half penny short. It is a fact which will be long remembered as remarkable down there, that she was never drowned, but died triumphantly in bed, at ninety–two. I have understood that it was, to the last, her proudest boast, that she never had been on the water in her life, except upon a bridge; and that over her tea (to which she was extremely partial) she, to the last, expressed her **indignation** at the impiety of mariners and others, who had the presumption to go 'meandering' about the world. It was in vain to represent to her that some conveniences, tea perhaps included, resulted from this objectionable practice. She always returned, with greater emphasis and with an **instinctive** knowledge of the strength of her objection, 'Let us have no meandering.'"

[**Source:** Extracted, with edits and revisions, from *David Copperfield* by Charles Dickens]

**5.1.** How is the tone of the passage?

(a) pensive

(b) **comic**

(c) depressing

(d) earnest

**5.2.** When was the author born?

(a) 10 o'clock on a Friday

(b) 12 o' clock on a Friday

(c) 11 o'clock on a Friday

(d) **midnight 12 o'clock on a Friday**

**5.3.** Which 'objectionable practice' does the writer refer to by "*It was in vain to represent to her that some conveniences, tea perhaps included, resulted from this objectionable practice?*"

(a) never going on the water

(b) the water in tea

(c) **the trips of the sailors**

(d) the visits upon the bridge

**5.4.** How many times was the caul auctioned?

(a) **once**

(b) twice

(c) thrice

(d) none of the above

**5.5.** What does the word 'reluctantly' mean according to the passage?

(a) warmly

(b) favourably

(c) **unwillingly**

(d) carefully

**5.6.** Most probably, the chapter seems to be-

(a) an excerpt of a story of the writer's caul auction

(b) an excerpt from the last chapter of a book

(c) **an excerpt from the first chapter of a book**

(d) a chapter of a book on natural science and related myths

**5.7.** Choose the word which is Most Similar to the word printed in bold in the passage:

**simultaneously**
(a) **100ᵗʰ anniversary**

(b) alternate
(c) closing
(d) none of the above


**5.8.** Choose the word which is Most Similar to the word printed in bold in the passage:
**inevitably**
(a) fair
(b) bad
(c) **primitive**
(d) collection


**5.9.** Choose the word which is Most Opposite to the word printed in bold in the passage:
**indignation**
(a) creation
(b) **variation**
(c) preparation
(d) sharing


**5.10.** Choose the word which is Most Opposite to the word printed in bold in the passage:
**instinctive**
(a) short
(b) dreadful
(c) **definite**
(d) vague

# PASSAGE-6

Dear Ashutosh,

Hope you are doing well!

I read your e-mail and got to know about your concern for improving your command on English language. I wish to express that if you'd like to improve your English, one thing you can do is to build up your vocabulary. In order to do this, you have to practice a lot. I'm afraid there is not a short cut for this. But there are many effective ways. First of all, you should read a lot. You can read short stories, comics, newspapers, magazines etc. depending on your English level. As you read, you can try to guess the meanings of unknown words from the context of the sentence. If you cannot, then look up the definition in a dictionary. English to English dictionary should be your first choice and keep the **translator** as last. Another way of building **vocabulary** is to watch movies in English which will also help with pronunciation. Try to be involved with the language as much as you can. Maintain a vocabulary notebook and write down a few words each day. Keep in mind that you have to revise them regularly. In my opinion, to communicate with people all you need is words. Even if you just say the words one after another, people most likely will understand what you mean regardless of the order of the words and grammatical construction.

Bye for now. Take care and try to practice the above mentioned suggestions in order to get positive results.

Dear Prakriti,

I'm better now. Thanks!

It's been a month I haven't heard from you. I hope you are well. Thanks for suggesting ways to improve my command on the language. I will surely try to work upon the suggestions given by you.

I must tell you, Prakriti that I had a **terrible** day at school yesterday. My friends and I were playing football in the school yard when I suddenly fell and twisted my ankle. At first I didn't experience much pain, but shortly it started hurting badly. I had difficulty walking so my friends helped me around. They took me to a hospital and stayed with me until my parents arrived. The doctor said it was broken and I needed to rest for a month. We came home last night and I feel better now. This unpleasant incident also made me realize how **valuable** friendships are. One needs a true friend for sure to be able to stay calm and get good advice. I don't know what I would do without them. So I want to say I feel happy to have excellent friends like you.

Do take good care of yourself and keep writing.



**6.1.** What is the objective of the e-mail drafted by Prakriti?

    a.  Difficulties of learning English
    (b) Problems of learning a second language alone
    (c) What's the best way of learning English
    (d) **What can we do to improve our English**

**6.2.** According to the first e-mail, which of the following is incorrect?

(a) We should read a lot
(b) We should take notes when we learn new words
(c) **We should use a translator for all the unknown words**

(d) We should practice as much as we can


**6.3.** What is the most important thing to communicate with people according to the writer?

(a) Grammar
(b) **Vocabulary**
(c) Order of the words used
(d) Advanced English course


**6.4.** Is watching English movies helpful in improving one's vocabulary in the language?
(a) Not at all
(b) **Yes**
(c) Not known

(d) Can't say


**6.5.** Which of the following is incorrect, according to the second e-mail?
(a) Ashutosh injured his ankle

(b) Ashutosh's friends helped him get to a hospital
(c) **Ashutosh hurt his arm**
(d) Ashutosh won't be able to go to school for a month


**6.6.** According to the second e-mail, what does Ashutosh want to emphasize in his e-mail?
(a) He should stop playing volleyball
(b) The terrible day he had
(c) The importance of school
(d) **The importance of friendship**

**6.7.** Choose the word which is Most Similar to the word printed in bold in the passage
**translator**
(a) **interpreter**
(b) dignitary
(c) manager
(d) none of the above


**6.8.** Choose the word which is Most Similar to the word printed in bold in the passage.

vocabulary
(a) language
(b) **lexicon**
(c) letters
(d) alphabet


**6.9.** Choose the word which is Most Opposite to the word printed in bold in the passage.
terrible
(a) dingy
(b) opposite
(c) **slight**
(d) flawless


**6.10.** Choose the word which is Most Opposite to the word printed in bold in the passage.
valuable
(a) **worthless**
(b) hearty
(c) mighty
(d) righteous

# PASSAGE-7

No society can ever function smoothly without having a structured system. By civil society is meant an entire array of organized groups and institutions that are independent of the state, voluntary, and at least to some extent self generating and self reliant. This encompasses non-governmental organizations, independent mass media, think tanks, universities, and social and religious groups. Civil society contributes to good governance by being an overseer- against human rights infringement and governance deficit, voice of the weaker sections' point of view, an agitated voice of aggrieved citizens, service provider to areas and people not reached by efforts by the officials, etc. Civil society groups may establish ties to political parties and the state, but they have got to hold on to their independence, and they do not **look for** political power for themselves.

As far as the Democratic societies are concerned, they, from the earliest times, have expected their governments to protect the weak against the strong. No 'era of good feeling' can justify discharging the police force or giving up the idea of public control over concentrated private wealth. Conversely speaking, it is evident that a spirit of self-denial and moderation on the part of those who hold economic power will significantly mitigate the demand for utter impartiality. Men are extra concerned about liberty and security than in an equal distribution of wealth. The extent to which Government must hinder with business, consequently, is not exactly measured by the extent to which economic power is concentrated into a few hands.

The **mandatory** degree of government intervention depends chiefly on whether economic powers are oppressively used, and on the inevitability of keeping economic factors in a bearable state of steadiness. But with the necessity of meeting all these dangers and threats to liberty, the powers of government are unavoidably augmented, whichever political party may be in office. The expansion of government is an obvious outcome of the growth of technology and of the problems that go with the use of machines and science. Since the government in our nation, must take on more powers to meet its problems, there is no way to conserve freedom other than by making democracy further potently dominant.

**7.1.** The advent of science and technology has increased the

    a.  tyranny of the political parties
    b.  chances of economic inequality
    c.  **powers of the government**
    d.  freedom of people

**7.2** Which of the following is NOT TRUE in the context of the passage?

    a.  civil society contributes to good governance
    b.  civil society is an entire array of organized groups and institutions that are

independent of the state

    a.  **civil society groups would never establish ties to political parties and the state**
    b.  all of the above

**7.3.** A spirit of moderation on the economically sound people would make the less privileged

a.   unhappy with their lot
b.   **clamor less for absolute equality**
c.   more interested in freedom and security
d.   unhappy with the affluent class

**7.4.** The growth of government is necessitated to

a.   **make the rich and the poor happy**
b.   curb the accumulation of wealth in a few hands
c.   monitor science and technology
d.   deploy the police force wisely

**7.5.** 'Era of good feeling' in second paragraph refers to

a.   time without government
b.   time of adversity
c.   **time of prosperity**
d.   time of police atrocities

**7.6.** 'Bearable state of steadiness' in the last paragraph may indicate

a.   an adequate number of police force
b.   a reasonable level of economic equality
c.   a reasonable check on economic power
d.   **a reasonable amount of government interference**

**7.7.** According to the passage, what do democratic societies expect of their government?

a.   to do nothing
b.   to maintain an autocratic rule
c.   **to protect the weak against the strong**
d.   to be quiet

**7.8.** Which of the following is what man is extra concerned about, according to the above passage?

a.   conscience
b.   demand and supply
c.   political gains
d.   **liberty and security**

**7.9.** Which of the following is the meaning of the phrase look for as used in the passage?

a.   **to search**

b.  leave

c.  discuss

d.  protest

**7.10.** Give the synonym of the word **mandatory** as used in the passage

a.  goodness

b.  extraordinary

c.  able

d.  **obligatory**

# PASSAGE-8

As is rightly said that, *An ounce of patience is worth a pound of brains* which lays prominence on the fact that persistence is far better than intelligence, by and large. Although, we do know that it's easily said than done as most of us fail to follow it the way we laud it.

In the current testing times of the Covid 19 situation, we see the significance of having endurance when we have no power over the circumstances. Nevertheless, having patience and controlling our feelings may do wonders as far as overcoming any such given depressing state of affairs are concerned. It depends completely on our mind-set as to whether we choose to whimper and complain or to wait for the right time patiently and remain calm and composed until the things get better.

Patience in this hour is the key apart from taking care of each other, helping the needy, doing our parts in fighting the virus by staying indoors and adhering to the covid appropriate behavioural norms.

The government bodies have a challenging job to keep us and this country safe. Let us not make their job more difficult by flouting the rules and containment measures.

As a matter of fact, one should always keep in mind the adage- *this too shall pass*! Therefore, instead of thinking that it's only me who is in distress and all others are having a gala time. One should, rather, understand that things are similar with others too; though, these could be at different point in time, in case of others. Consequently, it could be concluded that things would become simple if one merely accepts life and its challenges as they come. We shall, surely, defeat this crisis. Eventually, we will crush this viciously invisible enemy, and, are sure to beat it with a spirit of camaraderie and kindness to keep this nation protected and strong.

**8.1.** Which of the below most suitably explains the comment *an ounce of patience is worth a*

*pound of brains*:

    a. **Patience comes first, intelligence next**
    b. All the people are wise
    c. Patience is of no use
    d. Without patience, it's impossible to use intelligence completely

**8.2.** What does the following phrase imply- people consider other person's problems to be light and their own life full of obstacles and issues?

    a. They are self-centered
    b. They are baffled
    c. They get worried and sad
    d. **They feel that they alone face serious problems while others have a pleasant time**

**8.3.** Which of the following statements is TRUE according to the given passage?

a. Wisdom is of no use
b. Patience is mediocre
c. **Patience is far better than wisdom**
d. None of the above

**8.4.** Which of the following may do wonders as far as overcoming any given off-putting circumstances are concerned?

a. Scientific inventions
b. **Patience and controlling our thoughts**
c. Riches and authority
d. One's destiny

**8.5.** Which of the following is the most appropriate title for the given passage?

a. **This too shall pass**

b Patience is pretty hard to follow

c Busy people are tolerant

d Complicatedness and its solutions

# PASSAGE-9

The Dalai Lama's 86th birthday, celebrated on Tuesday, made headlines here for an unusual reason – PM Modi had greeted the Tibetan spiritual leader. The public acknowledgement is, of course, a subtle recalibration in the China policy as he's persona non grata for China. However, it also shows the limited number of cards India has as it confronts a belligerent China.

China recently celebrated the centenary of the Communist Party of China (CPC). India's challenge was amplified in the speech delivered by Xi Jinping. Its tenor signalled a China that will be even more confrontational. It poses a tricky challenge. Especially since commanders from the two militaries are scheduled to meet, for the 12th time, to work out a disengagement from friction points on the LAC in eastern Ladakh.

After China's unilateral ingress last year, in violation of existing border agreements, India negotiated disengagement this year at one friction point – Pangong Tso. However, there has been no progress on disengagement in Demchok, Gogra, Hot Springs and Depsang. China's actions and their scale have altered the bilateral relationship. GoI has begun to scale back the economic engagement. Noticeably, in keeping China out of the forthcoming 5G transition and parts of the tech market.

An important takeaway for India is that the size and the sophistication of the domestic economy matters in securing strategic interests. China's increasing belligerence has accompanied its growing economic clout that is backed by a $14.7 trillion GDP. As India works on its economic transformation, it should deepen its ties with Taiwan, a global leader in semiconductors. Deepening ties will simultaneously serve India's economic interests and send China a message. Being deferential to China's sensitivities won't help India's cause.

[**Source:***Confronting Xi: India should engage both the Dalai Lama and Taiwan* July 7, 2021, 10:29 PM IST TOI Edit in TOI Editorials, India. https://timesofindia.indiatimes.com/blogs/toi-editorials/confronting-xi-india-should-engage-both-the-dalai-lama-and-taiwan/]

**9.1.** According to the passage what does the following statement mean- 'persona non grata'?

    a.  **An unacceptable or unwelcome person**
    b.  Mentally unfit person
    c.  Selfless person
    d.  An old person

**9.2.** What did China recently celebrate?

    a.  Nothing
    b.  Not known
    c.  **The centenary of the Communist Party of China**
    d.  Dalai Lama's 86th birthday

**9.3.** What does the expression *bottleneck* refer to as used in the passage?

    a.  Christianity
    b.  Journalism

c. People using bottles

d. **Is a situation that stops a process or activity from progressing**

**9.4.** Which of the following statements as given in the above passage is TRUE?

a. All Refugees are inhuman

b. The Refugees need to be deserted

c. **The Refugees deserve a new lease on life**

d. We should neither be compassionate nor empathize with anybody

**9.5.** Which of the following words is the most OPPOSITE in meaning to *decree* as used in the passage?

a. **Request**

b) Rare

c) Experiment

d) Cancellation

# PASSAGE-10

I recently had to sign a big card - which is a horror unto itself, especially as the keeper of the Big Card was leaning over me at the time. Suddenly I was on the spot, a rabbit in the headlights, torn between doing a fun message or some sort of in-joke or a drawing. Instead overwhelmed by the innumerable options on hand, I decided to just write: "Good luck, best, Joe!"

To my shock, the next I found out that I had forgotten how to put my thoughts in writing. My entire way of life is "tap letters into computer". Even my shopping lists are hidden in the notes function of my phone. If I have to memorise something I immediately shoot an e-mail to myself. While under pressure to think, I chew a pen for better concentration. Paper is something I stack under my laptop to make it a more hassle-free height for me to type on with an ease.

Bic found by conducting an opinion poll of 1,000 teens by the stationers, that one in 10 don't possess a pen, a third have never written a letter, and half of 13 to 19 years old have never been forced to sit down and jot down even a thank you letter. More than 80% have never written a love letter, 56% don't have letter paper at home. And a quarter has never experienced the matchless agony of writing a birthday card. If at all a teen ever has used a pen is mainly on an exam paper.

Bic needs to recognize the changing priorities of the teens. Have you heard of smart phones, e-mail, face book and snap chatting? This is the future. Pens and Paper cease to exist. Handwriting is a relic.

"Handwriting is one of the most creative outlets we have and should be given the same importance as other art forms such as sketching, painting or photography."

[**Source:** Extracted, with edits and revisions, from https://www.jagranjosh.com/articles/ugc-net-reading-comprehension-questions-with-answers-1560863903-1]

**10.1.** When confronted with signing a big card, the author felt like "a rabbit in the headlight"

(first paragraph). What does this phrase mean?

    a.  **a state of confusion**
    b.  a state of pleasure
    c.  a state of anxiety
    d.  a state of pain

**10.2.** According to the author, which one is NOT the most creative outlet of pursuit?

    a.  photography
    b.  handwriting
    c.  sketching
    d.  **reading**

**10.3.** The primary purpose of the passage is most likely to

    a.  **express significance of writing**

b.  clarify the motivation behind an artist's work
c.  contrast sketching and photography
d.  getting confused while typing

**10.4.** The entire existence of the author revolves round:

a.  computer
b.  mobile phone
c.  typewriter
d.  **both (a) and (b)**

**10.5.** How many teens, as per the Bic survey, do not own a pen?

a.  800
b.  500
c.  130
d.  **100**

**10.6.** What is the main concern of the author?

a.  that the teens use social networks for communication
b.  that the teens use mobile phones
c.  that the teens use computer
d.  **that the teens have forgotten the art of handwriting**

**10.7.** Which of the following is NOT TRUE as per the second paragraph?

a.  **that the author writes extensively**
b.  that the author uses mobile even for making a shopping list
c.  that the author places a heap of papers under his laptop
d.  that the author doesn't enjoy writing

**10.8.** Choose the word which is most similar in meaning to **innumerable** as used in the

passage.

a.  similar
b.  **multifarious**
c.  descending
d.  social

**10.9.** Choose the word which is most opposite in meaning to the word outlet as used in the last paragraph of the given passage.

a.  despair

b. narrow
        c. out
        d. **ingress**

**10.10.** How many teens, as per the Bic survey, have never written a love letter?

        a. 100 per cent
        b. 1 per cent
        c. **More than 80 per cent**
        d. Less than 80 per cent

# CHAPTER THREE

# UG QUESTION PAPER FORMAT

**UG Question Paper Format**

a. Maximum Marks 150
b. Duration of CLAT 2022 Exam 02:00 Hours
c. Multiple-Choice Questions 150 questions of one mark each
d. Negative Marking 0.25 Mark for each wrong answer

**Subject Areas with weightage:**
(approximate number of questions)
English Language
28-32 questions, or roughly 20% of the paper
Current Affairs, including General Knowledge
35-39 questions, or roughly 25% of the paper
Legal Reasoning
35-39 questions, or roughly 25% of the paper
Logical Reasoning
28-32 questions, or roughly 20% of the paper
Quantitative Techniques
13-17 questions, or roughly 10% of the paper

# CHAPTER FOUR

# PG QUESTION PAPER FORMAT

**PG Question Paper Format**

a. Maximum Marks 120
b. Duration of exam 02:00 Hours
c. Multiple-Choice Questions 120 questions of one mark each
d. **Syllabus:**

1. Constitutional Law
2. Other areas of law such as Jurisprudence, Administrative Law, Law of Contract, Torts, Family Law, Criminal Law, Property Law, Company Law, Public International Law, Tax Law, Environmental Law, and Labour & Industrial Law

a. **Negative Marking**

0.25 Mark will be deducted for each wrong answer

# UG QUESTION PAPER 2022

**UG 2022**

**CONSORTIUM OF NATIONAL LAW UNIVERSITIES COMMON LAW ADMISSION TEST-2022**

## Five Year Integrated Law Programme

### INSTRUCTIONS TO CANDIDATES

*(This Booklet contains 44 pages of Question Paper including 2 blank pages for rough work.)*

### Duration of Test : 2 Hours (120 Minutes) Maximum Marks : 150

1. Separate carbonised Optical Mark Reader (OMR) Response Sheet is supplied along with this Question Booklet and the carbon copy has to be detached and taken by the candidates.
2. In case of any discrepancy in the question booklet (QB), please request the Invigilator for replacement of a fresh packet of QB with OMR. Do not use the previous OMR Response Sheet for a fresh booklet so obtained.
3. Candidates will not be given a second blank OMR Response Sheet under any circumstance. Hence, OMR Response Sheet shall be handled carefully.
4. Answer all questions. No clarification can be sought on the Question Paper.
5. Possession of Electronic Devices in any form is Strictly prohibited in the Examination Hall.
6. The use of any unfair means by any candidate shall result in the cancellation of his/her examination.
7. Impersonation is an offense and the candidate, apart from disqualification, will be liable to be prosecuted.
8. The Test Paper for Five Year Integrated Law Programme is for 150 marks containing 150 Multiple Choice Questions.
9. There will be Negative marking for multiple choice objective type questions. **0.25 marks** will be deducted for every wrong answer or where candidates have marked more than one response.

10. Use **BLACK/BLUE BALL POINT PEN** only for writing the Roll No. and other details on OMR Response Sheet.
11. Use **BLACK/BLUE BALL POINT PEN** for shading the circles. Indicate only **the most appropriate answer** by shading from the options provided. The answer circle should be shaded completely without leaving any space.
12. As the responses cannot be modified/corrected on the OMR Response Sheet, candidates have to take necessary precautions before marking the appropriate circle.
13. The candidate should retain the Admit Card duly Signed by the Invigilator, as the same has to be produced at the time of Admission.
14. Handle the OMR Response Sheet with care. Do not fold.
15. Ensure that Invigilator puts his/her signature in the space provided on the OMR Response Sheet. Candidate should sign in the space provided on the OMR Response Sheet.

16. The candidate should write Question Paper Booklet No., and OMR Response Sheet No., and sign in the space/ column provided in the attendance sheet.

17. Return the ORIGINAL Page of OMR Response Sheet to the Invigilator after the Examination.

18. The candidate shall not write anything on the OMR Response Sheet other than the details required and in the spaces provided for.

M1

---

### CONTENTS OF QUESTION PAPER

**Subject:** English Language
**Q. Nos.** 1 – 30
**Page No.** 3 – 11
**Subject:** Current Affairs and General Knowledge
**Q. Nos.** 31 – 65
**Page No.** 12 –18
**Subject:** Legal Reasoning
**Q. Nos.** 66 – 105
**Page No.** 19 – 32
**Subject:** Logical Reasoning
**Q. Nos.** 106 – 135
**Page No.** 33 – 40
**Subject:**
Quantitative Techniques
**Q. Nos.** 136 – 150
**Page No.** 41 – 42
**English Language**
   Text    Box:    English
Language

I. Public speaking is a powerful real-life skill. Over the centuries, impressive speeches made by people from various walks of life have helped to change hearts, minds and shape the world as we see it today. Speeches that are delivered with intense emotions and conviction can infuse compassion and forgiveness; elevate levels of hatred and destruction; break or unite nations.

On October 5, in 1877 in the mountains of Montana Territory, when Chief Joseph surrendered to General Nelson A. Miles, the former gave a *Surrender Speech*. The speech included these words: *"It is cold, and we have no blankets; the little children are freezing to death. I want time to look for my children, and see how many of them I can find. Maybe I shall find them among the dead. Hear me, my Chiefs! I am tired; my heart is sick and sad. From where the sun now stands I will fight no more forever."*

The heart-wrenching speech bared the grief and misery of the speaker, and those subjected to overwhelming hardships.

During World War II, the speech *We Shall Fight on the Beaches* delivered by Winston Churchill on June 4, 1940 is considered a high-powered speech that strengthened the determination of those present in the House of Commons. In the speech, he said, *"Even though large tracts of Europe and many old and famous States have fallen or may fall into the grip of the Gestapo and all the odious apparatus of Nazi rule, we shall not flag or fail. We shall go on to the end, we shall fight in France, we shall fight on the seas and oceans, we shall fight with growing confidence and growing strength in the air, we shall defend our island, whatever the cost may be, we shall fight on the beaches, we shall fight on the landing grounds, we shall fight in the fields and in the streets, we shall fight in the hills;"*

In 1950, William Faulkner was honoured with a Nobel Prize for his significant contributions to the American novel. This was the time when the Soviet Union had found the possible implications of the use of the atomic bomb, and people had begun to live in the fear of annihilation. In his *Nobel Prize Acceptance Speech*, Faulkner urged writers of various genres to think and write beyond the fear of destruction, and instead write materials that would lift the human spirit. The powerful message included: *"I believe that man will not merely endure: he will prevail. He is immortal, not because he alone among creatures has an inexhaustible voice, but because he has a soul, a spirit capable of compassion and sacrifice and endurance. The poet's, the writer's, duty is to write about these things. It is his privilege to help man endure by lifting his heart, by reminding him of the courage and honor and hope and pride and compassion and pity and sacrifice which have been the glories of his past. The poet's voice need not merely be the record of man, it can be one of the props, the pillars to help him endure and prevail."*

Undoubtedly, effective speeches have a long-lasting impact on the minds of the listeners, and they elevate the levels of awareness or actions the speaker intends to raise or catalyze.

1. The main idea of the passage is that

   A. All leaders should be accomplished public speakers.
   B. An impactful speech can convey a strong message to the listeners.
   C. A speech should sound pleasing to the ears of the listeners.
   D. Publicspeakers should be bold and argumentative.

2. The tone of the Surrender Speech is

   A. Satiric (B) Optimistic (C) Poignant (D) Narcissistic

3. It is evident that through his speech, Churchill wished to his countrymen .

   A. Inform, about the challenges that arise in a war-torn country.
   B. Warn, against the futility of war.
   C. Remind, how their endeavours to fight against the Nazi rule had failed miserably.
   D. Reassure, that they would combat fiercely against their enemy under all circumstances.

4. Which one of the following is the least likely to be used to describe Churchill?

   A. Resolute (B) Undaunted (C) Complacent (D) Unwavering

5. In the sentence : *'The poet's voice need not merely be the record of man, it can be one of the props, the pillars to help him endure and prevail'* Faulkner has used to convey the power of a poet's writings.

   A. A metaphor (B) A simile

(C) An onomatopoeia (D) A transferred epithet

II. As a six-year-old child-beggar, Saroo slept off in a stationary train in Khandwa, Madhya Pradesh; however, when he woke up, he found himself in an empty compartment of a train thundering towards Kolkata where he spent a couple of weeks in a state of panic and hopelessness. Finally, he ended up in a local government adoption centre from where he was adopted by an Australian couple. Twenty five years later, Saroo felt the urge to trace his biological mother and see in what state she lived. Relentlessly, he used Google's satellite feature to map the parts of the country that could have possibly been his own hometown. The search was a long and arduous one;

nevertheless, the perseverance did pay. One eventful day, he met his mother; thereafter, he continued to keep in touch with her.

If technology can unite people with their loved ones, it can also make them distant. The unlimited variety of applications (apps) available to toddlers, teenagers and adults might have revolutionized their lives for the better, but these very apps have snatched away the joys of long naturewalks; they have encroached upon the time and space that people earlier used for physical interaction; they have drilled deep chasms of loneliness in the lives of countless numbers of people.

Simple pleasures of life include visiting friends and relatives, playing matches in open spaces, interacting with people in markets, public libraries and clubs. However, with the escalating rage of using apps like those for social media, playing virtual games, and homedelivery services, these joyous moments are fading into oblivion, and the pall of loneliness is getting heavier by the day.

Where are we heading to? Are we going to allow ourselves to be swamped by apps? Are we going to allow socialmedia to engulf us in a deluge of loneliness and isolation? Are we going to drive ourselves to situations that will ultimately demand mental and physical therapies to regain normalcy? Do we not know that physical interaction is as essential for mental health as food and water is for physical health?

Earlier, social isolation was mostly experienced by some of the elderly people who were devoid of an occupation, and bereft of company of their loved ones. Unfortunately today, an unhealthy solitude prevails among numerous children, teenagers and adults too; subsequently, there is an alarming increase in the demand for mental health therapy practitioners.

The necessity of engaging psychologists in schools and colleges is evidently on the rise. The psychologists are required to identify and address the learning and behavioral needs of students who approach them for guidance; moreover, if required, the professionals are expected to help them in strengthening their emotional, social and academic skills.

Regardless how alarming the situation might be, it is never too late. If people revert to the earlier trend of shopping off-line, going for naturewalks, playing outdoors games, and catching up with friends in their homes or cafés more frequently, they can keep their heads firmly well above the ocean of loneliness.

6.  From the passage it is evident that Saroo's desire to find his mother

   A.  Ended up being a distant dream.
   B.  Inspired him to use Google's satellite feature intermittently.
   C.  Waned as time went by.
   D.  Did not slacken till he succeeded.

7.  In the sentence 'these very apps have snatched away the joys of long nature-walks;' the author has

   A.  Satirized nature (B) Metaphorized apps

(C) Personified apps (D) None of the above

8.  From the passage one can conclude that

   A.  It is impossible for people to reduce the usage of apps.
   B.  There is a direct correlation between loneliness and excessive usage of social- media apps.
   C.  The usage of technology is as essential for mental-health as food and water is for physical health.
   D.  All senior citizens are lonely because they are not tech-savvy.

9. From the passage it can be inferred that presently in many educational institutions

    A. The number of teachers who pass the buck to psychologists is on the rise.
    B. Special emphasis is being laid on the mental and emotional health of the students.
    C. The usage of educational apps is being discouraged significantly.
    D. All the students feel the need to be counseled by psychologists.

10. In the concluding paragraph of the given passage, the writer's tone can be best described as

    A. Optimistic (B) Despairing

(C) Laudatory (D) Apologetic

III. *"Wash! Wash! Wash your hands! "* That's been the safety-mantra ever since the pandemic COVID-19 began swamping the world. Undoubtedly, washing hands has proven to be the best way to keep germs at bay. Unfortunately, the medical practitioner who first promoted the importance of this simple activity was subjected to intense humiliation, and ultimately declared insane!

Ignaz Semmelweis was a Hungarian doctor. In 1847, as an obstetrician, he was disturbed that post-delivery, almost every third woman died of an unexpected malady. He observed that as a part of the set routine, medical students and doctors would examine and study the corpses in the mortuary, and then come for rounds to the maternity wards. Here, without washing their hands, they would examine expectant mothers. After making numerous hypothesis and observations, he was convinced that when doctors washed their hands before examining the women in the ward, the number of deaths due to serious infection declined. He shared his observations with his colleagues and many others working in the field of medicine, but unfortunately he could not provide any concrete evidence to his theory. Sadly, due to the vehement criticism that he received, he went into depression. Furthermore, Ignaz strived to prove his point so relentlessly that it led to the belief that he had lost his mind. In 1865, a doctor deceptively lured him into an asylum for the insane, and two weeks of the brutal treatment that was meted out to him by the attendants led to his untimely death. About twenty years later, when the world became more receptive to the works of scientists like Louis Pasteur and Joseph Lister, awareness regarding germs that cause diseases began to spread. This is the time when Ignaz was honoured with titles like *Father of Hand Hygiene* and *Saviour of Mothers*- an honour much too late!

Some of the most celebrated artists have earned fame much after their deaths. It is tragic that Vincent Van Gogh's awe-inspiring work was labeled as strange and amateur by most of the critics of his time. It is believed that he sold only one or two painting in his lifetime, and that too for a meager amount. Today, every single painting of Vincent Van Gogh paintings is worth millions of dollars.

Franz Kafka was a proficient writer, but when he published a few pieces of his writings, he received immense criticism. Before his death in 1924, he handed over his unpublished novels and short stories to his friend Max Brod, and urged him to destroy them; however, Brod got the manuscripts published. Today, Franz is acclaimed as one of the major fiction writers of the twentieth century; the novels titled *The Trial* published in 1925, and *The Castle* published in 1926 are considered two of his masterpieces.

Perhaps, if humans were more tolerant and amenable to change, innovative concepts, theories and creations, the deserving would live to experience the glory and honour they rightfully deserve.

11. The main idea of the passage is that

    A. All original theories and works should receive unreserved acceptance.
    B. Many undeserving innovators have been honoured after their demise.
    C. Creativity must never be inhibited.

    D.  Numerous innovators have found recognition and appreciation of their works posthumously.

12.  From the passage it is evident that Dr. Ignaz's theory was rejected because

    A.  He could not substantiate it
    B.  The doctors did not want him to regulate their work ethics
    C.  He had been declared insane
    D.  Joseph Lister and Louis Pasteur had already discovered germs

13.  From the passage one can conclude that the art critics who Van Gogh's works were .

    A.  Applauded, pessimistic.
    B.  Censured, hypercritical.
    C.  Denounced, tolerant.
    D.  Acclaimed, rigid.

14.  From the passage it can be inferred that Max Brod

    A.  Was of the opinion that Franz had not reached out to the right critics
    B.  Decried Franz's writings
    C.  Considered it unsacred to destroy any manuscript
    D.  Appreciated and valued Franz's works

15.  The word *relentlessly* in the passage can be best replaced by the word

    A.  Irresolutely (B) Recklessly

(C) Unabatedly (D) Unabashedly

IV.  Cryptocurrencies are a terrible thing. They are the essence of a Ponzi scheme whose value is based entirely on a greater fool prepared to buy it. The promise of alchemy-turning lead into gold has bewitched humanity throughout the ages and cryptocurrencies are just the latest alchemy. Do not get me wrong, if rich people want to lose their money, in this or any other way, they should be allowed to do so. The rich should be the vanguards of new things in case something unforeseen and good falls out of them. But we need to protect those vulnerable consumers whose lives are such that almost any get-rich-quick schemes will be seductive, and seven out of 10 times, they will lose their life savings. Cryptocurrencies are today's South Sea Bubble – one of the earliest recorded financial bubbles that took place in the 1720s' Britain. Meme-based currencies like Dogecoin, Dogelon Mars and Doge Dash remind me of the infamous plan of one company during the South Sea Bubble to raise money "for carrying on an undertaking of great advantage; but nobody to know what it is."

The cryptocurrency bubble is worse than tulip mania. Through the veil of technology, cryptocurrency enthusiasts are leaning on policy-makers to permit them to be exempt from regulation, privatize money, and make money so disconnected from the economy that it would reap financial disaster. There are many reasons to avoid financial disasters, but one of them is that they ratchet up poverty and inequality. The current money–credit system is not perfect, but like democracy, it is the worst system barring all the others. It has evolved from the ashes of the system cryptocurrency enthusiasts are trying to resurrect.

The current system is vulnerable to attack because money is little understood. Cryptocurrency enthusiasts have attracted a following based on the fiction that the central bank or government creates money and are busy debasing it in their self-interest. This is not the case, but then

again, there is some overlap between cryptocurrency advocates, conspiracy theorists, and *anti-vaxxers*. The time has come for someone to stand up for the current fiat money system and explain that while it could be better still, it has been associated with far more growth, much more distributed, and has responded better to economic crisis than what came before.

In today's money–credit system, banks create money when they issue a loan and place the loan's proceeds into the account of their customers, creating a deposit. Money is, in fact, a tradable debt. The bank's deposit can be used as cash because the bank is a regulated issuer of loans and deposit-taker, which gives the deposit credibility and convertibility. The central bank only influences the creation of money indirectly by its regulatory requirement that a proportion of the loans need to be funded by shareholder's profits. They need to have skin in the game. Money creation then is based on thousands of separate decisions by loan officers and is more distributed than a centralized algorithm like Bitcoin. And its supply is determined by the private demand for loans, which means it is closely aligned to the economy.

16. Which of the following does best describe attitude of the author towards rich people?

    A.  Concerned (B) Assiduous (C) Indifferent (D) Sympathetic

17. Which of the following is true in the context of the passage?

    A.  The author defends the current money–credit system.
    B.  The author rejects the idea that the central bank or government creates money and are busy debasing it in their self-interest.
    C.  The author backs the protection of poor from menace of cryptocurrencies.
    D.  All the above

18. Which rhetorical device is employed in 'cryptocurrencies are just the latest alchemy'?

    A.  Antithesis (B) Metaphor

(C) Personification (D) Synecdoche

19. Which of the following does best describe the passage?

    A.  Argumentative and explanatory (B) Descriptive and argumentative

(C) Narrative and explanatory (D) Expository and argumentative

20. What do the cryptocurrency enthusiasts rely on?

    A.  Exemption from regulation
    B.  Privatization of money
    C.  Disconnection of money from the economy
    D.  All the above

V.  The fact that Gaia, in her monstrous avatar, decided to distribute fossil fuels very unevenly across the Earth has been central to the emergence of the world's current geopolitical order. From a vitalist point of view, it could be said that the wars of the twentieth century were won as much by the fossilized energy of botanical matter as by particular groups of humans.

In the First World War Germany's lack of oil put it at a huge disadvantage against the Allies, more or less ensuring its defeat. The shortage of oil effectively cancelled the technological

advantages Germany enjoyed at the start of the war: despite having a large fleet, for instance, it was unable to use its navy effectively because its coal-burning ships needed to refuel every eleven days. Conversely, the assured supply of American oil conferred so great an advantage on Britain and France that "it could be fairly stated that the war was won for the Western allies by tankers." Not for nothing was it said of the First World War that Britain, France, and the United States floated "to victory on a sea of oil."

In the Second World War the shortage of oil was even more critical to the defeat of the Axis powers. The German Luftwaffe was forced to rely on synthetic fuels derived from coal, and these could not provide the high-octane energy that was necessary for high- compression aero engines: "it was largely due to the inferior engines in German aircraft that the Luftwaffe lost the Battle of Britain." The shortage of oil also dictated Germany's war strategy: it was in order to seize the oilfields of the Caucasus that the German army pushed eastward into the Soviet Union in 1942, leading to a defeat at Stalingrad from which it never recovered. Japan's invasion of the Dutch East Indies was similarly forced by its lack of oil.

In short, over the course of the twentieth century access to oil became the central focus of global geopolitical strategy: for a Great Power, to be able to ensure or hinder the flow of oil was to have a thumb on the jugulars of its adversaries. In the first part of the twentieth century the guarantor of the flow of oil was Britain. After the Second World War, the baton was passed, along with a string of British naval bases, to the United States. The role of guarantor of global energy flows is still crucial to US strategic dominance and to its position as global hegemon.

Today, as Elizabeth DeLoughrey has pointed out, "US energy policy has become increasingly militarized and secured by the Navy, the largest oceanic force on the planet." In the words of the historian Michael Klare, the Iraq War of 2003 marked the transformation of the US military into "a global oil protection service, guarding pipelines, refineries, and loading facilities in the Middle East and elsewhere."

It is important to note that the strategic value of controlling oil flows is tangentially related to the US's energy requirements. The period in which the American military was turning into "a global oil protection service" was one in which the US was well on its way to reducing its dependence on imported oil. The fact that the US is now self-sufficient in fossil fuels has in no way diminished the strategic importance of oil as an instrument for the projection of power- it is the ability to deny energy supplies to rivals that is strategically of central importance.

21.  What is the central idea of the passage?

    A.  Fossil fuels in war-making.
    B.  Strategic value fossil fuels in US dominance in the world.
    C.  Role of fossil fuels in modern geopolitical order.
    D.  Distribution of fossil fuels in the world.

22.  What was the cause of Germany's defeat in the First World War?

    A.  Germany's shortage of oil
    B.  Advantage of Britain and France
    C.  Weaknesses of Germany's navy
    D.  All the above

23.  Which of the following could be inferred from Michael Klare's opinion on US military?

    A.  The US military interferes with energy needs of other countries.

B.  The US energy policy has become increasingly militarized.
C.  The US has changed energy policy drastically.
D.  The US has fully understood the strategic value of controlling oil flows.

24.  What does the phrase 'tangentially related' to mean?

   A.  Related directly and in straightforward way
   B.  Related closely and centrally
   C.  Related only slightly and peripherally
   D.  None of the above

25.  What makes the US strategically dominating global hegemon?

   A.  Capacity of the US to provide oil protection service, guarding pipelines, refineries,

and loading facilities.

   B.  Increasingly militarized energy policy of the US Navy, the largest oceanic force on the planet.
   C.  The role of US as a guarantor of global energy flows.
   D.  All the above

VI.  The modern animal rights movement, which originated in the 1970s, may be understood as a reaction to dominant emphases within science and religion (principally, though not exclusively, Christianity). When the Jesuit Joseph Rickaby wrote in 1888 that "Brute beasts, not having understanding and therefore not being persons, cannot have any rights" and that we have "no duties of charity or duties of any kind to the lower animals as neither to stocks and stones", he was only articulating, albeit in an extreme form, the moral insensitivity that has characterized the Western view of animals.

That insensitivity is the result of an amalgam of influences. The first, and for many years the most dominant, was the "other worldly" or "world denying" tendency in Christianity, which has, at its worst, denigrated the value of earthly things in comparison with things spiritual. Traditional Catholicism has divided the world into those beings that possess reason and therefore immortal souls, and those that do not. Christian spirituality has not consciously been at home with the world of non-human creatures-either animal or vegetable. Classic accounts of eternal life as found in Augustine of Hippo, Thomas Aquinas, or John Calvin make little or no reference to the world of animals. Animals, it seems, are merely transient or peripheral beings in an otherwise wholly human-centric economy of salvation.

The second idea-common to Christianity, Judaism, and Islam-is that animals, along with vegetables and minerals, exist instrumentally in relation to human beings; they are made for human beings, even belong to human beings, as resources in creation. This idea predates Christianity and is found notably in Aristotle, who argues that "since nature makes nothing to no purpose, it must be that nature has made them for the sake of man". This idea, largely unsupported by scripture, was nevertheless taken over by Aquinas, who conceived of creation as a rational hierarchy in which the intellectually inferior existed for the sake of the intellectually superior.

Such instrumentalism, which features rationality as the key factor dividing human beings from "brute beasts," has in turn buttressed the third influence, namely the notion of human superiority in creation. Human superiority need not, by itself, have led to the neglect of animal life, but when combined with the biblical ideas of being made "in the image of God" and God's preferential choice to become incarnate in human form, some sense of moral as well as theological ascendancy was indicated. As a result, Christianity, and to a lesser extent Judaism, have been characterized historically by an overwhelming concern for humanity in creation rather than an egalitarian concern for all forms of God-given life. That humans are more important than animals, and that they self-evidently merit moral solicitude in a way that animals cannot, has become religious doctrine. Thus the Catechism of the Catholic Church maintains that "it is . . . unworthy to spend money on them [animals] that should as a priority go to the relief of human misery".

These influences have in turn enabled and justified the scientific exploration of the natural world and specifically the subjection of animals to experimentation. Francis Bacon pursued his scientific investigations in the belief that humanity should "recover that right over nature which belongs to it by divine bequest". René Descartes famously likened the movements of a swallow to the workings of a clock, and maintained that "There is no prejudice to which we are more accustomed from our earliest years than the belief that dumb animals think".

26. Jesuit Joseph Rickaby's articulation on animals may be termed as:

A. Eco-centric view of animals (B) Anthropocentric view of animals

(C) Ethnocentric view of animals (D) Androcentric view of animals

27. According to the author, how did Christianity contribute to insensitivity of the West towards animals?

A. It denigrated the value of earthly things in comparison with spiritual things.
B. It divided the world into beings with and without reason.
C. It propagated as if animals are transient or peripheral in human centric economy of salvation.
D. All the above.

28. Which of the following is closest to the meaning of the word 'instrumentalism' as used in the passage?

A. Pragmatism (B) Idealism

(C) Egalitarianism (D) None of the above

29. Which of the following is not true in the context of the passage?

A. Western philosophy and science are both under the influence of religion.
B. Western philosophical views on animals have been influenced by religious notions

about them.

C. Western religious notions on animals have justified subjection of animals to scientific experimentation.
D. Some of the scientific views on animals have been influenced by religious notions

about them.

30. It may be inferred from René Descartes' view that

A. It as irrational to assume that animals have awareness and some mental capacities.
B. Animals are automata or they act mechanically.
C. Neither (A) nor (B)
D. Both (A) and (B)

**Current Affairs and General Knowledge**
Text Box: Current Affairs and General Knowledge

VII. When we hear the name SPACE, only one organization comes to mind: the Indian Space Research Organization (ISRO). The Indian Space Research Organization (ISRO), located in Bengaluru, is the country's first space agency. ISRO was founded in 1969 with the goal of developing and utilizing space technology for national development while also conducting planetary exploration and space science research. The space research operations began in India in the early 1960s, at a time when satellite applications were still in the experimental stages in the United States. Dr. Vikram Sarabhai, the founding father of India's space programme, rapidly recognized the benefits of space technologies after the live transmission of the Tokyo Olympic Games across the Pacific by the American satellite 'Syncom-3' demonstrated the power of communication satellites. The ISRO has launched various spacecrafts like the Chandrayaan, Astrosat, Microsat, GSAT etc. The Government of India has also approved a regional spaceborne navigation system, which will consist of seven satellites. Out of these, four of them will be placed in geosynchronous inclined orbit of 29° relative to the equatorial plane. Such an arrangement would mean all seven satellites would have continuous radio visibility with Indian control stations.

31. Name the first dedicated mission launched by ISRO for studying the celestial sources

in X-ray, optical and UV spectral bands simultaneously.

   A.  Amazonia (B) Astrosat

(C) Gaganyaan – 1 (D) Lunar Polar Exploration Mission

32. APPLE, the first communication satellite of ISRO was launched from:

   A.  Satish Dhawan Space Centre, Sriharikota
   B.  TERLS, Thiruvananthapuram
   C.  Kourou, French Guiana
   D.  SSLV Launching Station, Tamil Nadu

33. Name the spacecraft that has been successfully sent into the space to probe into the planets in the solar system.

   A.  Sputnik 19 (B) Cosmos 482

(C) Pioneer-E (D) Mariner 10

34. The first successful Nuclear Bomb test conducted by India in 1974, is called the:

   A.  Prithvi (B) Pokhran-II

(C) Smiling Buddha (D) Surya

35. NaviC covers India and region extending:

(A) 1,500 Km (B) 2,000 Km
(C) 7,000 Km (D) 1,000 Km

VIII. On December 26, 2021, for the first time since the present government came to power in 2014, the Union Home Ministry constituted a panel led by its officers to review the withdrawal of the Armed areas. The Act was amended in 1972 and the powers to declare an area as "disturbed" were conferred concurrently upon the Central Government along with the States. Currently, the MHA issues periodic "disturbed area" notification to extend AFSPA only for Nagaland and Arunachal Pradesh, where it is applicable in the districts of Tirap, Changlang, Longding and areas falling under Namsai and Mahadevpur police stations bordering Assam. The notification for Manipur and Assam is issued by the State Governments. Tripura revoked the Act in 2015 and Meghalaya was under AFSPA for 27 years, until it was revoked by the MHA from April 1, 2018. The Act was implemented in a 20-km area along the border with Assam. Jammu and Kashmir has a separate J&K Armed Forces (Special Powers) Act, 1990.

36. Power to notify parts of or the whole of a State or a Union Territory as a 'disturbed area', under the Armed Forces (Special Powers) Act, 1958 is vested with:

   A. Governor of any State (B) Administrator of a Union Territory

   (C) Central Government (D) All of the above

37. AFSPA was introduced in Meghalaya in the year: (A) 1995 (B) 1999

   (C) 1991 (D) 1989

38. Consider the following statements about the Armed Forces (Special Powers) Act and mark the correct option.

   A. Detractors and Human Rights Organizations, as well as many sections of civil society, argue that the Act often leads to excesses and require checks and balances or could alienate the people instead of integrating them with the main stream.
   B. Irom Chanu Sharmila, an activist from Manipur, became ansensitizing figure symbolizing the protest against AFSPA after she sat on an indefinite fast in 2000, demanding its repeal and ended it only in August 2016.
   C. Both (A) and (B) are correct
   D. None of the above

39. In 2005, a government-appointed five-member committee, recommended that AFSPA be repealed. It suggested that the Unlawful Activities (Prevention) Act could be suitably amended to deal with terrorism. It made this recommendation as it felt that the AFSPA created an impression that the people of the Northeast States were being targeted for hostile treatment. Who headed this committee?

   A. B. P. Jeevan Reddy
   B. Abhishek Singhvi
   C. Soli Sorabjee
   D. Ram Jethmalani

40. AFSPA is currently in force in:

   A. Arunachal Pradesh and Assam
   B. Nagaland and Manipur
   C. Jammu and Kashmir

D. All of the above

IX. One of the justifications of Russia-Ukraine war Russian leader claimed that military action was necessary to stop Ukrainian attacks on the two break away regions of Donetsk and Lugansk, which Russia recognized as sovereign states. President of Russia claimed that Russia could come under attack by Ukrainian far right government, unless their influence in the country is diminished. He accused Western Nations of arming Kyiv against Russia. After being ordered by Russia's leader to invade the capital of Ukraine, Russian troops moved in several directions. As the first targets were hit, airports and the military HQs were located near cities across Ukraine, then tanks and troops rolled into the country from the north, east, and south. The war has demolished most of the cities of the Ukraine and caused irreparable damage to the humanity.

41. Ukraine was part of which country during 1922-1991?

A. Germany (B) Poland

(C) USA (D) USSR

42. Who is the President of Ukraine?

A. Volodymyr Zelenskyy (B) Vladimir Zelenskyy

(C) Volodymyr S. Zelenskyy (D) Vladimir Zelensky

43. Which is the currency of Ukraine?

A. Guilder (B) Zloty

(C) Ruble (D) Hryvnia

44. The President of Ukraine was formerly:

A. Weather Forecaster (B) Navy Officer

(C) Comedian (D) TV News Reader

45. Which operation was launched by the Indian Government to bring back Indians from Ukraine during Russia-Ukraine war?

A. Operation Kyiv (B) Operation Ganga

(C) Operation Rakshak (D) Operation East Star

X. Every second patent granted in India between 2016-2021 is related to green technology and a quarter of the green technology patents are concerning alternative energy production, coinciding with the Centre's efforts on *"enhanced use of green technology for boosting economy and encouraging consumers to use products produced through use of such technology"*. Data from the Ministry of Commerce and Industry shows that more than 91,500 patents were granted between 2016-17 and 2020-21, while the data for 2021-22 was not immediately available. However, going by the trend in the past two years, India is expected to clear at least 25,000 more applications this year.

Separate data from the ministry shows that between 2016-17 and 2021-22 (up to January), 61,186 patents related to green technologies have been granted in the said period. Of these, 90% are for technologies concerning waste management and alternative energy production- 38,837 or 63% of them are related to waste management and more than 16,000 or 26% are for alternative energy production. The rest of the green technology patentsare for energy conservation (2,555),transportation technologies (2,481),nuclear power generation (1,079),agriculture-and-forestry (161),and others (69).

46. With which country India entered into a 'Green Strategic Partnership' in September 2020?

   A. Poland (B) Greece

(C) Denmark (D) South Korea

47. In pursuance of the United Nations Sustainable Development Goals (SDG), India aims to be energy independent by the year

(A) 2047 (B) 2040
(C) 2045 (D) 2057

48. According to the Global Innovation Index 2021 published by the World Intellectual Property Organization (WIPO), India is ranked out of 132 countries.

   A. 45th (B) 46th

(C) 47th (D) 48th

49. In January 2022, the Union Cabinet approved the second phase of the Green Energy Corridor (GEC) in India with the objective to facilitate

   A. Grid integration and power evacuation of Renewable Energy (RE) Power Projects in seven States.
   B. Ecologically sustainable growth by increasing carbon footprint.
   C. Ecologically sustainable production of fossil fuels.
   D. Spreading awareness regarding Renewable Energy (RE) Power Projects.

50. The IRENA is an intergovernmental organization that supports countries in their transition to a sustainable energy future and serves as the principal platform for international co-operation on renewable energy. IRENA stands for:

   A. Intergovernmental Renewable Energy Association
   B. International Renewable Energy Association
   C. Intergovernmental Renewable Energy Agency
   D. International Renewable Energy Agency

XI. The Government may defer the deadline for companies to deposit the unspent portion of their Corporate Social Responsibility (CSR) funds into specified bank accounts in a move aimed at providing some relief in the fight against the COVID-19 and subsequent restrictions. Companies are required to spend at least 2% of their average net profit of the preceding within three financial years on CSR. The Ministry has allowed firms to undertake projects on an ongoing basis on the condition that any unspent amount must be deposited with a scheduled bank within 30 days of the end of the financial year. *"Considering the current crisis, we request your esteemed office to consider relaxation by providing extension of the timelines up to June 30, 2021,"* the Institute of Company Secretaries of India said in a letter to the Ministry. Experts said that while lockdowns and restrictions are less stringent than last year and companies have adapted to working online, many professionals or their families have been affected by the infection, leaving teams short-staffed.

51.  Which of the following is the Corporate Social Responsibility (CSR) initiative of the erstwhile Facebook India to promote women entrepreneurship?

A.  Shakti (B) Pragati

(C) Lean In (D) Marching Forward

52.  In 2019, which of the following Committees recommended that CSR expenditure should be made tax deductible expenditure?

A.  Company Laws Committee
B.  High Level Committee on Reform of Indian Company Law
C.  High Level Committee on Corporate Social Responsibility
D.  Committee for Reforms in Corporate Social Responsibility in India

53.  CAWACH is an initiative by the National Science and Technology Entrepreneurship Development Board, Department of Science and Technology, Government of India stands for the:

A.  Centre for Alleviating Waning Healthcare Companies
B.  Centre for Augmenting Wound-up Healthcare Companies
C.  Centre for Augmenting WAR with COVID-19 Health Crisis
D.  Centre for Alleviating Withering Healthcare Companies

54.  On January 22, 2021 the Companies (Corporate Social Responsibility Policy)

Amendment Rules, 2021 were notified by the:

A.  Ministry of Finance
B.  Ministry of Social Justice and Empowerment
C.  Ministry of Law and Justice
D.  Ministry of Corporate Affairs

55.  The Ministry of Corporate Affairs has instituted an award to select companies to recognize corporate initiatives in the area of Corporate Social Responsibility (CSR) to achieve inclusive growth and inclusive and sustainable development. The name of the award is:

A.  National Corporate Social Responsibility Awards
B.  National Awards for Excellence in Social Responsibility
C.  National Awards for Corporate Excellence in Social Responsibility
D.  National Awards for Excellence in Inclusive Growth and Sustainable Development

XII. With the announcement of Drone Shakti in the Union Budget, the industry got a massive push after the liberalization of the Drone Rules in 2021. The Government stated that start-ups will be promoted to facilitate Drone Shakti, with 'drone as a service'.

*"The current Government has taken a serious paradigm shift on drone technology and Drone Shakti announcement of the current FY budget proves the government's clear vision and focus towards this emerging industry. Drone Shakti and Kisan Drones will definitely help get this technology to impact common people on the grassroots level at a massive scale,"* according to the founder and CEO of a prominent aerospace quoted in a business magazine. The country is set to witness the use of large, unmanned aircraft systems weighing more than 150 kilograms across the sectors. Kisan Drones are already being used for crop assessments, land records, spraying of insecticides, and are expected to boost a wave of technology in the Agri and farming sector. Drones are also being used in surveillance systems for Railway Security. In India, drones were also deployed to deliver COVID-19 vaccines.

56. COVID-19 vaccines were delivered by drones as ICMR-led pilot project to:

   A.  Ladakh (B) Katra

   (C) Dantewada (D) Manipur

57. Which of the following is the online platform hosted by the Directorate General of Civil Aviation for various activities related to the management of drone activities in India?

   A.  e-Drone Shakti (B) Digital Sky platform

   (C) Aakash Shakti (D) Digital Drone platform

58. Which of the following refers to the phenomenon of restricting the movement of drones

within a defined airspace?

   A.  Geo-fencing (B) Drone-fencing

   (C) Sky-fencing (D) Air-fencing

59. The Drone Rules, 2021 have been made in supersession of which of the following rules?

   A.  The Unmanned Aircraft System Rules, 2020
   B.  The Aircraft Rules, 2020
   C.  The Unmanned Aircraft System Rules, 2021
   D.  The Manned Aircraft Rules, 1934

60. Which autonomous body is responsible for national accreditation structure for drones?

   A.  Drone Council of India (B) Unmanned Aircraft Council of India

   (C) Manned Aircraft Council of India (D) Quality Council of India

XIII.   The 21ˢᵗ century has seen an overall shift in India's policy outlook and also the global outlook towards India. Coherent policy initiatives and effective implementation on the ground have ensured a positive growth profile. The biggest shift has been the recognition of the maritime sector. Somehow, post-independence, we as a nation became sea blind and completely undermined our maritime potential. Initially, the Indian Navy came out with their Military

Maritime Strategy in 2007, titled "Freedom to use the Seas". They kept on upgrading their vision document on regular intervals with latest being declared in 2015. The Security And Growth for All in the Region (SAGAR) vision declared by the Government of India in May 2015 has been a massive game changer on multiple fronts. It integrates the geopolitical and geostrategic realities to domestic requirements. The security concerns and the blue economic opportunities are comprehensively addressed along with the diplomatic leverage and reviving the rich maritime heritage.

The SAGAR vision has been backed by aggressive push by the Government of India to drive mega projects with massive human resource requirements.

61.   Which of the following is the flagship programme of the Ministry of Shipping, Government of India, to promote port-led development in the country through harnessing India's 7,500 km long coastline, 14,500 km of potentially navigable waterways and strategic location on key international maritime trade routes?

   A.   Sagarmala Programme (B) Sagarshakti Programme

   (C) Jalshakti Programme (D) Jalmala Programme

62.   Which of the following is the initiative of the Ministry of Earth Sciences (MoES), Government of India, to explore marine resources and develop deep sea technologies for sustainable use of ocean resources?

   A.   Sagarmanthan Mission (B) Samudramanthan Mission

   (C) Deep Ocean Mission (D) Deep Ocean and Sea Technology Mission

63.   ISA is a United Nations body regulating the exploration and exploitation of marine non-living resources of oceans in international waters. ISA stands for:

   A.   International Sea Authority (B) International Sea Association

   (C) International Seafaring Association (D) International Seabed Authority

64.   Under Mission SAGAR, which Indian Naval Ship was deployed by the Indian Navy to provide humanitarian and medical assistance to Maldives, Mauritius, Seychelles, Madagascar and Comoros?

   A.   INS Kesari (B) INS Vikrant

   (C) INS Viraat (D) INS Vikramaditya

65.   Which of the following is India's first manned ocean mission which was launched at

Chennai?

A.  Samudrashakti (B) Samudrayan

(C) Sagaryan (D) Sagarshakti

**Legal Reasoning**

Text      Box:      Legal
Reasoning

XIV.  Writ is a public law remedy. It refers to a formal, written order issued by a judicial authority directing an individual or authority to do or refrain from doing an act. The High Court, while exercising its power of judicial review, does not act as an appellate body. It is concerned with illegality, irrationality and procedural impropriety of an order passed by the State or a Statutory Authority. A High Court is empowered to issue directions, orders or writs for the enforcement of Fundamental Rights and for any other purpose. The writ jurisdiction of High Court is discretionary and equitable. Writ of mandamus is issued by a court commanding a public authority to perform a public duty belonging to its office. It can be issued only when a legal duty is imposed on the authority and the petitioner has right to compel the performance of such duty. Writ of mandamus is requested to be issued, *inter alia*, to compel performance of public duties which may be administrative, ministerial or statutory in nature. A writ of mandamus may be issued in favour of a person who establishes a legal right in himself. It may be issued against a person who has a mandatory legal duty to perform, but has failed or has neglected to do so. Such a legal duty emanates by operation of law. The writ of mandamus is most extensive in regards to its remedial nature. The object of mandamus is to prevent disorder emanating from failure of justice and is required to be granted in all cases where law has established no specific remedy.

66.  The government of a state made a rule to make it discretionary to grant dearness allowance to its employees. One of the employees filed a writ petition seeking a mandamus to compel the government to grant dearness allowance. In the given situation, which of the following statements is true?

A.  Writ of mandamus cannot be granted as no legal duty was imposed on the government to grant dearness allowance.

B.  Writ of mandamus cannot be granted as a statutory right was conferred on the employee to receive dearness allowance.

C.  Writ of mandamus can be granted as it is a public law remedy.

D.  Writ of mandamus can be granted as it is a discretionary remedy.

67.  A public-spirited citizen filed a writ petition seeking a mandamus to compel the government to make a law to curb the ill-effects of climate change. In the given situation, which of the following statements is true?

A.  Writ of mandamus can be granted as it is an equitable remedy.

B.  Writ of mandamus cannot be granted as no legal duty is imposed on the government to pass a law to curb the ill-effects of climate change.

C.  Writ of mandamus can be granted as it is a discretionary remedy.

D.  Writ of mandamus cannot be granted as there is no violation of fundamental right.

68.  Mr. A and Mr. B are parties to a contract of sale of goods. Upon breach of contractual obligations by Mr. A, Mr. B filed a writ petition seeking a mandamus to compel Mr. A to perform his obligations under the contract. In the given situation, which of the following statements is true?

A.  Writ of mandamus can be granted as it is a discretionary remedy.

B.  Writ of mandamus cannot be granted as there is no violation of fundamental right.

C.  Writ of mandamus cannot be granted as Mr. B's right under the contract is a private right.

D.  Writ of mandamus can be granted as there is no statutory duty imposed on

Mr. A to fulfill his contractual obligations.

69.  A licensing officer is under a statutory duty to issue a license to an applicant who fulfils the conditions prescribed for the issue of such license. Mr. X, an applicant, fulfilled all the conditions prescribed for the issue of such license, but his application for issuance of license was rejected by the licensing officer. In the given situation, which of the following statements is correct?

A.  Writ of mandamus can be granted compelling the license officer to issue the

license.

B.  Writ of mandamus cannot be granted compelling the license officer to issue the

license as there is no violation of fundamental right.

C.  Writ of mandamus can be granted as it is the discretion of the licensing officer to

grant license.

D.  Writ of mandamus cannot be granted compelling the license officer to issue the

license as there is no violation of public duty.

70.  Which of the following statements is incorrect?

A.  Writ of mandamus may be issued in favour of a person who establishes the existence of a legal right.

B.  Writ of mandamus may be issued against a person or authority who has a mandatory duty to perform but has failed or has neglected to do so.

C.  Writ of mandamus is purported to prevent disorder emanating from failure of justice.

D.  Writ of mandamus may be requested to be issued to compel performance of private duties which may be administrative, ministerial or statutory in nature.

XV.  To maintain the secular character of the Indian polity, not only does the Constitution of India guarantee freedom of religion to individuals and groups, but it is also against the general policy of the Constitution of India that any money be paid out of the public funds for promoting or maintaining any particular religion. Accordingly, it is provided in the Constitution of India that no person shall be compelled to pay any taxes, the proceeds of which are specifically appropriated in payment of expenses for the promotion or maintenance of any particular religion or religious denomination. This does not prohibit the State from enacting a law to incur expenses for the promotion or maintenance of any particular religion or religious denomination, but by such law, no person can be compelled to pay any tax, the proceeds of which are to be so utilized. This, however, does not invalidate levy of a fee to provide some service. Thus, a fee can be levied on pilgrims to a religious fair to meet the expenses of the measures taken to safeguard the health, safety and welfare of the pilgrims. Such fee levied by a State will be valid because the object of such contribution is not to foster or preserve religion, but to control secular administration of religious institutions.

71. Mr. A, a tax-payer of various taxes levied by the State Government, filed a writ petition for issuance of a writ of mandamus directing the State to forbear from spending any amount from the public funds of the state for renovation of water tanks belonging to a Hindu temple in the State. These tanks were used by the general public, irrespective of their religious affiliation, for bathing and drinking purposes. In the given situation, which of the following statements is correct?

    A. The State is promoting or maintaining the Hindu religion.
    B. The State cannot be said to be promoting or maintaining the Hindu religion.
    C. The State is compelling citizens to pay tax for promotion of Hindu religion.
    D. The State is compelling citizens to pay tax for maintenance of Hindu religion.

72. Communal riots between religion 'A' and religion 'B' resulted in the destruction of places of worship of both religions in a State. As a result, the State Government utilized public funds for restoring the places of worship of both religions 'A' and 'B'. In the given situation, which of the following statements is correct?

    A. The State Government's act is violative of the Constitution of India as it is promoting or maintaining particular religions.
    B. The State Government's act is not violative of the Constitution of India as it is not promoting or maintaining any particular religion.
    C. The State Government's act is violative of freedom of religion as it condones communal violence.
    D. The State Government's act is not violative of the Constitution of India as it is promoting or maintaining a particular religion.

73. Communal riots between religion 'A' and religion 'B' resulted in the destruction of a place of worship of religion 'B' in the State. As a result, the State Government utilized public funds for restoring the places of worship of religion 'B'. In the given situation, which of the following statements is correct?

    A. The State Government's act is violative of the Constitution of India as it is promoting or maintaining a particular religion.
    B. The State Government's act is not violative of the Constitution of India as it is promoting or maintaining a particular religion.
    C. The State Government's act is not violative of the Constitution of India as it is not promoting or maintaining a particular religion.
    D. The State Government's act is violative of freedom of religion as it condones communal violence.

74. A State Government passed a law making it mandatory for all residents of the State to pay a hefty 'pilgrimage tax' so as to aid the State in organizing a popular religious pilgrimage in that State. The said pilgrimage is undertaken only by followers of religion 'X' and draws a large number of followers of religion 'X' from all over the country to the state every year. In the given situation, which of the following statements is correct?

    A. The State Government's act is violative of the Constitution of India as it is not promoting or maintaining religion 'X'.
    B. The State Government's act is not violative of the Constitution of India as it is not promoting or maintaining religion 'X'.
    C. The State Government's act is violative of the Constitution of India as it is compelling citizens to pay tax for promoting or maintaining religion 'X'.
    D. The State Government's act is not violative of the Constitution of India as it is a measure to safeguard the health, safety and welfare of the pilgrims.

75. The object of a State Legislation is "to provide for the better administration and governance of certain Hindu religious endowments", where 'religious endowment' means the property belonging to or given or endowed for the support of temples. The State Legislation vests the supervision of public temples in a statutory authority, i.e., 'Commissioner of Hindu Religious Endowments'. For the purpose of meeting the expenses of the Commissioner and his staff, every Hindu temple in the State is required under provisions of the State Legislation, to pay an annual contribution at certain percentage of their annual income. In the given situation, which of the following statements is correct regarding the annual contribution provided under the State Legislation?

   A. It is not violative of the Constitution of India because its object is the proper administration of religious trusts and institutions.
   B. It is not violative of the Constitution of India because its object is fostering of Hindu religion.
   C. It is violative of the Constitution of India because its object is fostering of Hindu religion.
   D. It is violative of the Constitution of India because its object is not inclusive of administration of religious endowments belonging to all religions.

XVI. The Constitution of India guarantees to all its citizens certain fundamental freedoms, which are recognized as their fundamental rights. However, these fundamental freedoms guaranteed by the Constitution of India are not absolute as no right can be. Each of these fundamental rights is liable to be controlled, curtailed and regulated to some extent by laws made by the Parliament or the State Legislatures. Accordingly, the Constitution of India lays down the grounds and the purposes for which a legislature can impose 'reasonable restrictions' on the rights guaranteed to citizens. The State cannot travel beyond the contours of these reasonable restrictions in curbing the fundamental rights guaranteed to citizens. While determining the constitutional validity of a restriction imposed on a fundamental right by a legislation, the Court is not concerned with the necessity of the restriction or the wisdom of the policy underlying it, but only whether the restriction is in excess of the requirement, and whether the legislature has overstepped the Constitutional limitations. Two of the fundamental rights guaranteed to every citizen of India are- the right to move freely throughout the territory of India and the right to reside and settle in any part of India. However, the State may impose reasonable restrictions on these rights by law, in the interests of the general public or for the protection of the interests of any Scheduled Tribes.

76. A law was enacted by the Parliament of India which consisted of a provision making it mandatory for every person riding a two-wheeler in India, to wear a helmet, failing which such person was made liable to a fine. Mr. X, a citizen of India, was fined for violation of the said provision. Mr. X challenged the constitutional validity of the said provision. In the given situation, which of the following statements is correct?

   A. The provision is violative of the Constitution of India because it is a restriction on the freedom to move freely throughout the territory of India.
   B. The provision is not violative of the Constitution of India because it is a reasonable restriction on the freedom to move freely throughout the territory of India.
   C. Mr. X's fundamental right to move freely throughout the territory of India is violated.
   D. Both (A) and (C).

77. A group of Indian students of XYZ University located in New Delhi, India posted on social networking sites that they would hold a demonstration outside the university campus, protesting against a recently passed law which made it compulsory for university students to wear uniforms while attending classes. The students further threatened to "use whatever means necessary" to "stop the oppression of students". Therefore, the State Authorities placed barricades around the university campus in order to restrict movement of the students carrying out the demonstration and ensuring that the demonstration does not turn violent. In the given

situation, which of the following statements is correct regarding the act of placing of barricades by State Authorities?

A. The act is violative of the Constitution of India because it is a restriction on the freedom to move freely throughout the territory of India.
B. The act is not violative of the Constitution of India because it is a reasonable restriction in the interests of general public.
C. The act is violative of the Constitution of India because it is restriction in the interest of students.
D. The act is not violative of the Constitution of India because it is a reasonable restriction in the interest of morality.

78. The appropriate authority in a State passed an externment order against Mr. A, a citizen of India. The externment order prohibited Mr. A, from residing within the State, from the date specified in such order. The externment order was passed by virtue of powers conferred on the appropriate authority by law, and the constitutional validity of this law had been upheld by the Supreme Court of India. The externment order was passed on the ground that Mr. A was found to be frequently engaged in illegal business of narcotic drugs and was also involved in several cases of riot and criminal intimidation. In the given situation, which of the following statements is correct regarding the externment order?

A. It is a reasonable restriction on Mr. A's fundamental right of free movement throughout the territory of India.
B. It is an unreasonable restriction on Mr. A's fundamental right of residence and settlement in any part of India.
C. It is violative of Mr. A's fundamental right of free movement throughout the territory of India.
D. It is an unreasonable restriction on Mr. A's fundamental right of free movement throughout the territory of India.

79. Mr. Z, a citizen of India, was issued a passport on June 1, 2020 by the Passport Office. Mr. Z was due to travel to Spain on July 15, 2021. On July 11, 2021, Mr. Z received a letter from the Regional Passport Officer intimating him that it was decided by the Government of India to seize his passport "in public interest". Mr. Z was required to surrender his passport within seven days of the receipt of that letter. In the given situation, which of the following statements is correct?

A. Mr. Z can challenge the letter on the ground that it is violative of his fundamental right of free movement throughout the territory of India.
B. Mr. Z can challenge the letter on the ground that it is violative of his fundamental right to reside and settle in any part of India.
C. Mr. Z can challenge the letter on the ground that it is violative of the law relating to passports in India.
D. Mr. Z cannot challenge the letter on the ground that it is violative of his fundamental right(s) of free movement throughout the territory of India and/or to residence and settlement in any part of India.

80. Which of the following statements is incorrect?

A. Fundamental right to movement and residence in any part of India are sacrosanct and are guaranteed to all citizens.
B. Fundamental right to movement and residence in any part of India are sacrosanct, but are guaranteed subject to reasonable restrictions on such rights.

    C.  Reasonable restrictions may be imposed, on fundamental rights to movement and residence in any part of India, by law.

    D.  The constitutional validity of a law imposing reasonable restrictions on fundamental rights can be challenged by a citizen before the legislature.

XVII.  Where a spouse contracts a second marriage while the first marriage is still subsisting, the spouse would be guilty of the offence of bigamy under the penal law in India, if it is proved that the first as well as the second marriages were legally valid, i.e., all the necessary ceremonies required by law or by custom have been performed at the time of contracting the marriages. According to the penal law in India, if a person, who has a living husband or wife, marries again, then such person is liable to be punished with imprisonment up to seven years along with a fine for committing the offence of bigamy. Although the penal law of India is applicable to all citizens irrespective of their religious affiliations, an exception to the offence of bigamy may be created by the law relating to marriage applicable to followers of a particular religion. Under the Hindu law relating to marriage, bigamy is not permitted. If a Hindu wife files a criminal complaint against her husband on the ground that during the subsistence of her marriage, her husband had married a second wife by converting into another religion which legally permits having more than one wife, then her husband is liable to be punished for the offence of bigamy. Further, the Hindu law relating to marriage also provides that the punishment for offence of bigamy as provided in the penal law of India would be applicable to marriage between two Hindus.

81.  Mr. A, a Hindu male, has been married to Ms. B, a Hindu female. Their marriage was solemnized as per Hindu rites and ceremonies. After his marriage to Ms. B, Mr. A underwent religious conversion into a religion 'X' which legally permits males to have two wives. Thereafter, Mr. A got married to Ms. C, a female belonging to religion 'X', in compliance with all the legal requirements of contracting a valid marriage under religion 'X'. In the given situation, which of the following statements is true?

    A.  As Mr. A married Ms. C, the marriage of Mr. A and Ms. B has become invalid.

    B.  As Mr. A is not a Hindu, the marriage of Mr. A and Ms. B has become invalid.

    C.  Mr. A's marriage with Ms. C has not affected the validity of his marriage with Ms. B.

    D.  Both (A) and (B).

82.  Mr. A, a Hindu male, has been married to Ms. B, a Hindu female. Their marriage was solemnized as per Hindu rites and ceremonies. After his marriage to Ms. B, Mr. A underwent religious conversion into a religion 'X' which legally permits males to have two wives. Thereafter, Mr. A got married to Ms. C, a female belonging to religion 'X', in compliance with all the legal requirements of contracting a valid marriage under religion 'X'. Ms. B filed a criminal complaint against Mr. A for committing the offence of bigamy. In the given situation, which of the following statements is true?

    A.  Mr. A is liable to be punished according to the Hindu law relating to marriage.

    B.  Mr. A is liable to be punished according to the penal law of India.

    C.  Mr. A has not committed the offence of bigamy.

    D.  Both (A) and (B).

83.  Mr. A, a Hindu male, has been married to Ms. B, a Hindu female. Their marriage was not solemnized as per Hindu rites and ceremonies or any other custom, but was performed by seeking blessings of their family members. After his marriage to Ms. B, Mr. A underwent religious conversion into a religion 'X' which legally permits males to have two wives. Thereafter, Mr. A got married to Ms. C, a female belonging to religion 'X', in compliance with all the legal requirements of contracting a valid marriage under religion 'X'. Ms. B filed a criminal complaint against Mr. A for committing the offence of bigamy. In the given situation, which of the

following statements is true?

A. Mr. A has committed the offence of bigamy because he married again during the

subsistence of the first marriage.

B. Mr. A has not committed the offence of bigamy because his first marriage is not

valid.

C. Mr. A has committed the offence of bigamy because he underwent religious conversion in order to contract a bigamous marriage.
D. Mr. A has not committed the offence of bigamy because his second marriage is not valid.

84. Mr. A, a male belonging to religion 'P', has been married to Ms. B, a female belonging to religion 'P'. Their marriage was solemnized in compliance with all the legal requirements of contracting a valid marriage under religion 'P'. Monogamy is espoused as a cherished value by the followers of religion 'P' and provided as a pre-condition for a valid marriage for the followers of the religion. After his marriage to Ms. B, Mr. A underwent religious conversion into a religion 'Q' which legally permits males to have two wives. Thereafter, Mr. A got married to Ms. C, a female belonging to religion 'Q', in compliance with all the legal requirements of contracting a valid marriage under religion 'Q'. Ms. B wife filed a criminal complaint against Mr. A for committing the offence of bigamy. In the given situation, which of the following statements is true?

A. Mr. A has committed bigamyaccording to the Hindu law relating to marriage.
B. Mr. A has committed bigamyaccording to the penal law of India.
C. Mr. A has committed bigamyaccording to the law relating to marriage of religion 'P'.
D. Both (B) and (C).

85. Which of the following statements is incorrect?

A. Marrying again during lifetime of husband or wife is a pre-condition for performing a valid Hindu marriage.
B. Religious conversion is not a defence for the offence of bigamy under the penal law of India.
C. Bigamy is an offence under the penal law of India.
D. Offence of bigamy can be committed according to the provisions of Hindu law relating to marriage.

XVIII. A special marriage, i.e., a marriage between persons from two different religious affiliations can be legally contracted in India under the provisions of the law relating to special marriages. The law relating to special marriages provides for the registration of such marriages and for divorce in such cases. One of the modes in which a special marriage can be legally terminated is through divorce by mutual consent of parties to the marriage. In order to obtain a divorce by mutual consent, both the parties to the special marriage are required to jointly present a petition for divorce to the district court on the ground that they have been living separately for one year or more, that they have not been able to live together and that they have mutually agreed that the marriage should be dissolved. At least six months after the presentation of such petition, but not later than eighteen months after the presentation of such petition, the district court, after hearing the parties and after making the necessary inquiry, and being satisfied that the marriage is a 'special marriage', and that the claims made in the petition are true, shall declare the marriage to be dissolved. Further, the personal presence of the parties before the district court at the time of presenting the joint petition for divorce is not mandatory, as the parties can satisfy the court even by affidavit that the requirements for granting divorce on mutual consent are fulfilled.

86. Ms. A, a Hindu female and Mr. B, a Christian male, got married as per the law relating to special marriages in January 2018. On January 26, 2021, Ms. A and Mr. B jointly presented a petition for divorce by mutual consent before the district court on the ground that they have been inflicting mental cruelty on each other for a period of three years and that they have mutually agreed that the marriage should be dissolved. In the given situation, which of the following statements is correct?

    A. The district court shall pass a decree of divorce within six months after the presentation of petition for divorce by mutual consent.
    B. The district court shall pass a decree of divorce after eighteen months of the presentation of petition for divorce by mutual consent.
    C. The district court shall not immediately pass a decree of divorce by mutual consent.
    D. The district court shall immediately pass a decree of divorce by mutual consent

if it is satisfied that the marriage was valid.

87. Ms. A, a Hindu female and Mr. B, a Christian male, got married as per the law relating to special marriages in January 2018. On February 15, 2021, Ms. A presented a petition for divorce by mutual consent before the district court on the ground that Ms. A and Mr. B have been living separately for a period of one year because Mr. B has been in an adulterous relationship with Ms. X, a Christian female. In the given situation, which of the following statements is correct?

    A. The district court shall pass a decree of divorce by mutual consent six months after the date of presentation of petition for divorce.
    B. The district court shall pass a decree of divorce by mutual consent eighteen months after the date of presentation of petition for divorce.
    C. The district court shall not pass a decree of divorce by mutual consent as the

requirements for grant of divorce are not fulfilled.

    D. The district court shall not pass a decree of divorce by mutual consent as Ms. A and Mr. B have not been living separately for more than one year.

88. Ms. A, a Hindu female and Mr. B, a Christian male, got married as per the law relating to special marriages in January 2018. On April10, 2021, Ms. A and Mr. B jointly presented a petition for divorce by mutual consent before the district court on the ground that they have been living separately for a period of three years and that they have mutually agreed that the marriage should be dissolved. In the given situation, which of the following statements is correct?

    A. The district court shall pass a decree of divorce by mutual consent after all other

legal requirements are fulfilled.

    B. The district court shall pass a decree of divorce by mutual consent immediately because Ms. A and Mr. B have been living separately for more than one year.
    C. The district court shall not pass a decree of divorce by mutual consent because the marriage between Ms. A and Mr. B is not valid.
    D. The district court shall not pass a decree of divorce by mutual consent because neither party is at fault in the marriage.

89. Ms. A, a Hindu female and Mr. B, a Christian male, got married as per the provisions of the law relating to special marriages in January 2018. On June16, 2021, Ms. A and Mr. B jointly presented a petition for divorce by mutual consent before the district court on the ground that they have been living separately for a period of three years and that they have mutually agreed that the marriage should be dissolved. During the presentation of the petition, while Ms. A was present physically in the district court, Mr. B joined via video-conferencing. In the given situation, which of the following statements is correct?

   A. The district court may pass a decree of divorce by mutual consent six months after the date of presentation of petition for divorce.

   B. The district court shall pass a decree of divorce by mutual consent after all other

legal requirements are fulfilled.

   C. The district court shall not pass a decree of divorce by mutual consent.

   D. Both (A) and (B).

90. Ms. A, a Hindu female and Mr. B, a Christian male, got married as per the law relating to special marriages in January 2018. On March15, 2021, Ms. A and Mr. B jointly presented a petition for divorce before the district court on the ground that they have been living separately for a period of three years and that they have mutually agreed that the marriage should be dissolved. Six months later, the district court, after hearing the parties and making inquiry, found that the marriage had been solemnized under the law relating to special marriages, and that the consent of Ms. A for the presentation of petition of divorce was obtained by fraud. In the given situation, which of the following statements is correct?

   A. The district court shall pass a decree of divorce by mutual consent because the

legal requirements are fulfilled.

   B. The district court shall pass a decree of divorce because the marriage had been solemnized under the law relating to special marriages.

   C. The district court shall not pass a decree of divorce because there was no mutual consent between parties.

   D. The district court shall not pass a decree of divorce because Ms. A has not been punished for fraud.

XIX. There are two principal theories on the relationship between international law and domestic law- Monism and Dualism. The monistic theory maintains that the subjects of two systems of law, i.e., international law and municipal law are essentially one. The monistic theory asserts that international law and municipal law are fundamentally the same in nature, and arise from the same science of law, and are manifestations of a single conception of law. The followers of this theory view international law and municipal law as part of a universal body of legal rules binding all human beings, collectively or singly. In a monist system, international law does not need to be incorporated into domestic law because international law immediately becomes incorporated in domestic legal system upon ratification of an

international treaty. According to this theory, domestic law is subordinate to international law. The Statute of the International Criminal Court, therefore, can be directly applied and adjudicated in national courts according to the monistic theory. According to dualism theory, international law and municipal law represent two entirely distinct legal systems, i.e., international has an intrinsically different character from that of municipal law. International law is not directly applicable in the domestic system under dualism. First, international law must be translated into State legislation before the domestic courts can apply it. For example, under dualism, ratification of the Statute of the International Criminal Court is not enough-it must be implemented through State legislation into the domestic system. Most states and courts presumptively view national and international legal systems as discrete entities and routinely discuss in dualist fashion incorporation of rules from one system to the other.

91. In light of the given passage, which of the following statements is correct?

    A. Monism and Dualism are similar approaches to adopt international law into domestic law.
    B. Dualism postulates the homogeneousness of domestic law and international law.
    C. Monism and Dualism are different approaches to understand how domestic law impacts international law.
    D. Monism postulates the homogeneousness of international law and domestic law.

92. 'X' is a developing country. 'X' ratified the United Nations Framework Convention on Climate Change in 1995, and incorporated the provisions of the said convention in its domestic legislation addressing climate change in 1996. However, 'X' has been widely criticized in the international community for its failure in meeting the obligations under the said convention. 'Y' is a developed country. 'Y' ratified the United Nations Framework Convention on Climate Change in 1995, and has not incorporated the provisions of the said convention in its domestic legislation till date. 'Y' has been appreciated by the international community for its success in meeting the obligations under the said convention. In the given situation, which of the following statements is correct?

    A. 'X' is a monist State and 'Y' is a dualist State.
    B. 'X' is a dualist State and 'Y' is a monist State.
    C. 'X' and 'Y' are both monist States.
    D. 'X' and 'Y' are both dualist States.

93. 'D', a dualist State, has signed and ratified the Agreement on Trade-related Aspects of Intellectual Property Rights (TRIPS Agreement), an international agreement administered by the World Trade Organization (WTO). If 'D' is compelled to fulfill its international obligations under the TRIPS Agreement, which of the following statements is correct?

    A. 'D' may adopt the provisions of the TRIPS Agreement without enacting a new domestic legislation or amending an existing legislation.
    B. 'D' may not incorporate the provisions of the TRIPS Agreement into a new domestic legislation.
    C. 'D' must incorporate the provisions of the TRIPS Agreement into an existing domestic legislation or in a new domestic legislation.
    D. 'D' may not incorporate the provisions of the TRIPS Agreement into an existing domestic legislation.

94. Which of the following statements is incorrect?

    A. According to monism, the nature of domestic law and international law is the same and domestic law is subordinate to international law.
    B. According to monism, ratified international conventions automatically become a

part of domestic law and domestic law is subordinate to international law.

    C. According to dualism, ratified international conventions automatically become a

part of domestic law and domestic law is subordinate to international law.

    D.  According to dualism, the nature of domestic law and international law is different and domestic law is not subordinate to international law.

95.  The country 'X' has ratified an International Convention which requires each State Party to enact laws defining and punishing bribery, i.e., the act of offering bribes to Government officials. The Convention has neither defined bribery, nor prescribed a punishment for the same, so that each State Party may define the offence of bribery differently in their respective domestic legislations. By 2022, 'X' has not enacted any law defining and punishing the offence of bribery. In November 2021, Mr. A was being prosecuted by a domestic criminal court in 'X' for allegedly offering a bribe to a Government official. In the given situation, which of the following statements is correct?

    A.  If 'X' is a monist State, Mr. A can be punished for committing an offence under the Convention.
    B.  If 'X' is a dualist State, Mr. A can be punished for committing an offence under the Convention.
    C.  If 'X' is a dualist State, Mr. A cannot be punished for committing an offence under the Convention.
    D.  Mr. A cannot be punished for committing an offence under the Convention irrespective of whether 'X' is a monist or a dualist State.

XX.  The United Nations Commission on Environment and Development defines 'sustainable development' as follows: *"Sustainable development is the development that meets the needs of the present without compromising the ability of future generations to meet their own needs."* Sustainable development clearly postulates an anthropocentric bias, least concerned with the rights of other species which live on this earth. Anthropocentrism is always human-interest focused thinking that considers non-humans as having only instrumental value to humans,

in other words, humans take precedence and human responsibilities towards non-human are based on benefits to humans. Eco-centrism is nature-centred, where humans are part of nature and non-humans have intrinsic value. In other words, human interest does not take automatic precedence and humans have obligations towards non-humans independently of human interest. Eco-centrism is, therefore, life-centred, nature-centred where nature includes both humans and non-humans. The Constitution of India protects not only human rights but also casts an obligation on human beings to protect and preserve a specie from becoming extinct. Conservation and protection of environment is an inseparable part of the fundamental right to life. According to the doctrine of 'public trust' recognized under the Constitution of India, certain common properties such as rivers, seashores, forests and the air are held by the Government in trusteeship for the free and unimpeded use of the general public. The resources like air, sea, waters and the forests have such a great importance to the people as a whole, that it would be totally unjustified to make them a subject of private ownership. The State, as a custodian of the natural resources, has a duty to maintain them not merely for the benefit of the public, but for the best interest of flora and fauna, wildlife and so on.

96.  Ms. G, a student of environmental science, has cultivated a butterfly garden which provides a favourable habitat for butterflies. Ms. G has cultivated the butterfly garden so that she could observe and study the different stages of development of butterflies such as egg, larvae, pupae, and adult. In the given situation, which of the following statements is correct?

    A.  Ms. G's approach to cultivation of butterfly garden is anthropocentric because it

concerns the furtherance of her academic interest.

    B.  Ms. G's approach to cultivation of butterfly garden is anthropocentric because it

concerns the conservation of environment.

    C.  Ms. G's approach to cultivation of butterfly garden is eco-centric because it concerns the provision a favourable habitat to the butterflies.

    D.  Ms. G's approach to cultivation of butterfly garden is eco-centric because it concerns the understanding of the different stages of development of butterflies.

97.  Which of the following statements is correct?

    A.  Anthropocentrism and eco-centrism are different approaches to achieving sustainable development.

    B.  Anthropocentrism focuses on the promotion of non-human interests.

    C.  Eco-centrism is concerned with the promotion of both human and non-human interests.

    D.  Anthropocentrism and eco-centrism are different approaches to protection of environment and sustainable development.

98.  Which of the following is the basis for the difference between anthropocentrism and eco-centrism?

    A.  The inherent value placed on humans and non-humans.

    B.  The inherent value placed on living things and non-living things.

    C.  The relationship between human society and environment.

    D.  The relationship between non-humans and environment.

99.  Which of the following statements is correct regarding fundamental right to life under the Constitution of India?

    A.  It creates a corresponding duty on human beings to protect and preserve non-humans.

    B.  It creates a corresponding duty on non-humans to protect the right to life of human beings.

    C.  It is inclusive of the right of human beings to utilize non-human resources to the best of their advantage.

    D.  It is inclusive of the right of non-humans to utilize human resources to the best of their advantage.

100.  Which of the following statements is incorrect according to the doctrine of 'public trust'?

    A.  Private ownership of forests is unwarranted.

    B.  Forests are held by the State in a fiduciary capacity.

    C.  State is obligated to maintain forests for their economic value.

    D.  State is obligated to maintain forests in the interest of humans and non-humans.

XXI.  When parties to a contract are under a 'mistake' regarding an important fact related to such contract, it may affect the contract in two ways. It may, firstly, defeat the consent altogether that the parties are supposed to have given, that is to say, the consent is unreal. Two or more persons are said to consent when they agree upon the same thing in the same sense. Secondly, the mistake may mislead the parties as to the purpose which they had contemplated. Where the mistake does not defeat consent, but only misleads the parties, i.e., where both parties to an agreement are under a mistake as to a matter of fact essential to the agreement, the agreement is void. However, if the mistake is concerning an erroneous opinion regarding value of the subject-matter of the agreement, it is not a mistake as to a matter of fact. Thus, agreement is void when: (1) both the parties to an agreement are mistaken, (2) their mistake is as to a matter of fact, and (3) the fact about which they are mistaken is essential to the agreement. Further, it is pertinent to note that a mistake, in order to invalidate a contract, should be a mistake of fact and not a mistake of law. Furthermore, where only one party to the contract is under mistake of fact, and the other party is not, the contract is not voidable merely for such reason.

101. Mr. A entered into an agreement to sell his bicycle which had been kept unused in his attic for a year, to Mr. B, at an agreed price. However, neither party was aware that at the time of entering into the agreement, the bicycle had already been destroyed by a fire in the attic. In the given situation, which of the following statements is true?

    A. The agreement is void as both parties were under a mistake as to a matter of fact essential to the agreement.
    B. The agreement is void as both parties were under a mistake as to a law in force in India.
    C. The agreement is not voidable as only one of the parties was under a mistake as to a matter of fact.
    D. The agreement is not voidable as the promise made under the agreement had not been performed.

102. Ms. X and Ms. Y entered into a contract of sale of an article, while reeling under the erroneous belief that the sale of the article, which was the subject-matter of the agreement, was permitted by the law in force in India. In the given situation, which of the following statements is true?

    A. The contract is valid.
    B. The contract is voidable at the option of Ms. X.
    C. The contract is voidable at the option of Ms. Y.
    D. The contract is not voidable.

103. Mr. J entered into an agreement with Mr. K for the sale of Mr. J's 'club'. At the time of entering into the agreement, while Mr. J believed that he was agreeing to sell his golf club, Mr. K believed that he was agreeing to buy a clubhouse owned by Mr. J. The agreement is void because:

    A. Mistake of fact defeated the consent of the parties.
    B. Mistake of fact misled the parties as to the purpose of the contract.
    C. Mistake of fact was regarding the identity of parties.
    D. Both (A) and (B)

104. Mr. D appointed Mr. K to manage the cultivation of his land as he was unable to manage it himself due to his advanced age. Mr. K agreed to manage the cultivation of Mr. D's land if he granted Mr. K a lease of the said land. Mr. D agreed to the same and signed a deed which was, unknown to both parties, a gift deed of the land and not a lease deed. In the given situation, which of the following statements is true?

    A. Mr. D and Mr. K were reeling under a mistake as to a matter of fact essential to the agreement.
    B. Mr. D and Mr. K were reeling under a mistake as to a matter of law essential to the agreement.
    C. Mr. D was reeling under a mistake as to a matter of fact essential to the agreement.
    D. Mr. D was reeling under a mistake as to a matter of law essential to the agreement.

105. Ms. X and Ms. Y entered into a contract of sale of an article which was agreed to be shipped by Ms. X in a ship named 'The Cruiser' and delivered to Ms. Y on an agreed date. Mr. X shipped the said article by a different ship named 'The Mariner', without informing Ms. Y and the article was delivered to Ms. Y on the agreed date. In the given situation, which of the following statements is true?

    A. The agreement is void as both parties were under a mistake as to a matter of fact essential to the agreement.
    B. The agreement is void as both parties were under a mistake as to a law in force in India.
    C. The agreement is valid as both parties were under a mistake as to a matter of fact not essential to the agreement.
    D. The agreement is valid as both parties were under a mistake as to a matter of fact essential to the agreement.

**Logical Reasoning**

Text Box: Logical Reasoning

XXII. Students decide to attend college for several reasons. These reasons include career opportunities and financial stability, intellectual growth, a time for self-discovery, norms, obligations, and social opportunities. Outside demands in society, such as technology changes, and increased educational demands also drive the need for more students to attend college. The students then spend the next few years trying to discover a path and find their way so they can become successful. The transition to college presents students with many new challenges, including increased academic demands, less time with family members, interpersonal problems with roommates and romantic interests, and financial stress. Competitive academic work and uncertainty about future employment and professional career were also noted as sources of stress. The transition to college represents a process characterized by change, ambiguity, and adjustment across all of life's domains. The transition towards independence and self-sufficiency has been characterized as 'stress-arousing' and 'anxiety-provoking' by many college students. Failure to accomplish and develop these characteristics of development and maintain independence may result in life dissatisfaction. Emerging adulthood has also been noted to augment college students' vulnerability to stress. Many students experience their first symptoms of depression and anxiety during this time, but a growing problem is that college campuses do not have enough resources to help all of these students. It has been noted that 75% to 80% of college students are moderately stressed and 10% to 12% are severely stressed.

106. What according to you is the objective of the study of the present paragraph?

    A. To map the various stages of pressure points of adulthood in the process of education.
    B. To narrate the anti-family agenda in the current education system.
    C. To pinpoint the obstacles targeted against meritorious students.
    D. All of the above

107. Which factors as per the author cause more stress amongst college students?

    A. Pressure from parents and society towards greater educational needs and increased competitive academic work.
    B. Failure to develop successful romantic interests, financial constraints and interpersonal issues with roommates.
    C. Failure to adapt to the transition to college life and to adjust various life domains in tune with needs and requirements of college life.
    D. Inability to manage time constraints and the uncertainty pertaining to their future.

108. Which of the following fall closest to the underlying assumption in the present study?

    A. Problem-solving ability amongst college students is negatively associated with symptoms of depression and anxiety.
    B. Students lean towards unhealthy coping skills in order to try to lower the stress that they experience.
    C. Romantic interest is an anti-dote for stress amongst the students in the colleges.
    D. Stress is subjective for each student.

109. Suggest a suitable title for the paragraph from amongst the given titles:

    A.  Triumph and Turbulence of College Education System
    B.  Negative impact of College Education System
    C.  Negligence of Stress Management by parents
    D.  Unemployment and Mental Instability

110.  With reference to the above paragraph, which of the following offers the most plausible solutions as a coping up mechanism for college students?

    A.  Individual students should approach counsellors for coping up with stress.
    B.  Keeping in view that large number of students are experiencing stress, colleges must take steps reduce course curriculum and peer pressures.
    C.  College authorities shall provide access to counselling and every student experiencing stress must engage in some form of coping mechanism to alleviate stress.
    D.  The students must learn to differentiate between short term and long-term stress.

XXIII.  Under the COVID-19 outbreak, universities and schools around the world had suspended face-to-face classes to prevent the rapid spread of the virus among students and staff. This sudden disruption to face-to-face education reshaped pedagogical practices and led to the rapid adoption of online teaching among universities. Subsequently, academics working at universities, at the frontline of those changes, faced enormous levels of pressure and disturbance to their professional roles and practices. For those without sufficient knowledge or experience for effective online teaching, this sudden transition was particularly challenging. In normal circumstances, designing an online course follows a systematic instructional design process with careful consideration of the unique characteristics of target learner groups and the chosen instructional medium. During the rapid adoption of online teaching in response to COVID-19, however, systematic instructional design procedures and team-based support for course development and preparation were unavailable. Instead, individual academics were given the challenge alone to teach online with a limited level of support and guidance from their school or university – the task was even more difficult in this situation where they were remotely working from home.

111.  The objective behind the information furnished in the passage is:

    A.  To examine the experiences faced by the teachers because of the sudden transition

from offline to online mode of teaching due to outbreak of COVID-19.

    B.  To identify the differences between the online and offline mode of teaching.
    C.  To reveal the side-effects of COVID-19.
    D.  To understand the need to be able to cope up with crisis like situations even in the educational sector.

112.  Based on the ideas presented in the paragraph, it will not be possible to draw out useful recommendations for situations like the pandemic, unless :

    A.  The factors required to contribute to quality education by online and offline modes

are examined.

    B.  Knowledge about the infrastructural availability in the schools or universities is crucial.
    C.  The faculty is given adequate training and experience in providing online education is taken into consideration.

   D.   A detailed analysis of the comparative performance in the online and offline modes

is done.

113.   What can be most conveniently inferred from the given paragraph?

   A.   Whether online or face-to-face, university teaching activity is a genuinely complex task that involves multiple elements of interlinked activity systems.

   B.   It has been more challenging for both individual academics and institutions to quickly adopt to online teaching during the COVID-19 Pandemic.

   C.   The object of the online teaching activity systems created a fundamental contradiction with the object of the previous teaching activity systems.

   D.   All the above.

114.   What suitable policy decision should be devised by the administrators of the schools and the universities, in the light of the facts presented in the paragraph?

   A.   There must be an insight into the complexity of online teaching and need to work for the capacity building of the teachers during such extra ordinary times and there is a greater need to create a teacher community and foster collaborative teaching relationships among the members, even if it takes time.

   B.   The faculty members must be oriented towards the lasting changes brought about to their roles and identities in teaching.

   C.   It is time to develop a comprehensive understanding of the challenges experienced by individual academics and the changes created by those academics.

   D.   There is a need to develop infrastructure in schools and universities.

115.   Which of the following points most closely supports the fact that the present education system lacks the structure to sustain effective teaching during and after the periods of lockdowns?

   A.   There are inadequate applications and platforms for effective online teaching.

   B.   Shift from offline to online was faced with resistance.

   C.   The academia's long-established roles and identities have been completely altered by the pandemic.

   D.   The students are interested in online examinations and schools and universities

are finding it difficult to shift to offline examination mode.

XXIV.   Biodiversity is being lost at a rate not seen since the last mass extinction. But the United Nations decade-old plan to slow down and eventually stop the decline of species and ecosystems by 2020 has failed. Most of the plan's 20 targets - known as the Aichi Biodiversity Targets - have not been met. The Aichi targets are part of an international agreement called the UN Convention on Biological Diversity, and member states are now finalizing replacements for them. Currently referred to as the post-2020 Global Biodiversity Framework (GBF), its draft was published in July 2021. It aims to slow down the rate of biodiversity loss by 2030. And by 2050, biodiversity will be *"valued, conserved, restored and wisely used, maintaining ecosystem services, sustaining a healthy planet and delivering benefits essential for all people"*. The GBF is a comprehensive plan. But success will require systemic change across public policy. That is both a strength and a weakness. If systemic change can be implemented, it will lead to real change. But if it cannot, there's no plan B. This has led some researchers to argue that one target or number should be prioritized and defined in a way that is clear to the public and to policy makers. It would be biodiversity's equivalent of the 2°C climate target.

116. As per the passage, which of the following is a challenge for implementation of the post-2020 Global Biodiversity Framework (GBF)?

    A. Unfulfillment of the pre-2020 global biodiversity targets
    B. Clarity of action plan for the society and government
    C. Threat of mass extinction
    D. Failure of plan to save ecosystems

117. According to the passage, why do some researchers advocate that one biodiversity target be prioritized?

    A. Systemic policy change is difficult to implement
    B. Post-2020 Global Biodiversity Framework (GBF) is comprehensive
    C. The 2 °C climate target needs to be prioritized
    D. Biodiversity needs to be valued, conserved, restored and wisely used

118. Which of the following is correct expression of the author's opinion as stated in passage?

    A. Implementation of the post-2020 Global Biodiversity Framework (GBF) allows no middle ground for success or failure.
    B. It is high time that countries re-evaluate the progress in achieving biodiversity targets.
    C. Biodiversity conservation should be prioritized over climate change at the global level.
    D. The post-2020 Global Biodiversity Framework (GBF) is the best way to prevent mass extinction.

119. Which of the following is the central theme of the above passage?

    A. The reason for failure of biodiversity conservation efforts at global level
    B. The inter-relationship between biodiversity conservation and climate change
    C. The future of biodiversity conservation efforts at global level
    D. The role of United Nations in biodiversity conservation at global level

120. Which of the following can be inferred from the above passage?

    A. The holistic nature of the post-2020 Global Biodiversity Framework (GBF) is a boon.
    B. The holistic nature of the post-2020 Global Biodiversity Framework (GBF) is a bane.
    C. The holistic nature of the post-2020 Global Biodiversity Framework (GBF) can be a boon or a bane.
    D. The post-2020 Global Biodiversity Framework (GBF) includes the 2°C climate target.

XXV. An unintended and unjust consequence of the Protection of Children from Sexual Offences Act, 2012 is its widespread persecution of teenage lovers. This law raised the age of consent from 16 to 18 years, while defining persons below 18 years as children. Consequently, when two 16-year-olds are romantically and sexually involved, but the girl's family doesn't approve the affair and files a police complaint, her consent has zero legal validity. And the consensual relationship morphs into a case of statutory rape. The Allahabad High Court has indicated how its "conscience" is concerned by such severe POCSO provisions being drawn by teenage lovers simply on the basis of family disapproval. The High Courts of Delhi, Madras and others have made similar observations in recent years and also pointed to amendments to the law that can help reduce its injustices. One suggestion that has gathered broad support is to push back both the cut-off for childhood and the age of consent to 16 years. Given that the NCRB data shows around half of POCSO cases falling in the 16-18 years age group, such an amendment is overdue. Minimizing the prosecution of consensual romances would also leave a logjammed system with more space to pursue actual sexual assault cases. The broader goal here is respecting the rights of adolescents and young adults. Their romantic and sexual autonomy needs greatly increased recognition in India.

121. *"Minimising the prosecution of consensual romances would also leave a logjammed system with more space to pursue actual sexual assault cases."*
In the context of the statement, which of the following strengthens the author's opinion?

    A. There are many unreported sexual assault cases.
    B. Speedy prosecution of sexual assault cases is desirable.
    C. Consensual romance, in some cases, can amount to sexual assault.
    D. Sexual assault and rape are different.

122. What has the author conveyed regarding the prosecution of statutory rape in India?

    A. Statutory rape does not violate the romantic and sexual autonomy of young adults.
    B. Statutory rape must be met with stricter punishment.
    C. Statutory rape must be abolished.
    D. Statutory rape is a relic of Victorian morality.

123. As per the above passage, which of the following does not correctly represent the author's view regarding the widespread persecution of teenage lovers under the POCSO Act?

    A. Teenagers have the right to love as much as adults.
    B. Police complaints of teenage lovers may lead to their harassment.
    C. Consent of minor girls do not have legal validity.
    D. Consent of minor girls have legal validity.

124. In the above passage, which of the following has concerned the "conscience" of the Allahabad High Court?

    A. Carelessness of teenage lovers.
    B. Threat to the safety of teenage lovers.
    C. Impact on mental health of teenage lovers.
    D. Harassment of teenage lovers by their families.

125. As per the above passage, which of the following is a major challenge in implementation of the POCSO Act?

    A. Speedy prosecution of cases.
    B. Respecting the rights of adolescents and young adults.
    C. Counselling of adolescents and young adults.
    D. Imposition of stringent punishment.

XXVI. A Madras High Court Judge's suggestion to amend the Constitution of India mandating that every citizen also has a duty to laugh comes as a whiff of fresh air – something the country has been gasping for, of late. Justice GR Swaminathan of the Madurai Bench has a remarkably refined sense of humour, but in quashing an FIR against a man arrested for an innocuous social media post, his insightful observations only highlight the idiocy and absurdity that surround the growth and normalisation of the offence-taking tribe. Written from the perspective of cartoonists and satirists, the judgment draws attention to how what ought to be a reasonable understanding of a situation is increasingly being influenced by impulses that border on the irrational and amount to an abuse of the legal process. The petitioner tried tongue-in-cheek wordplay while captioning photographs after a sightseeing trip with family : 'Trip to Sirumalai for shooting practice'. For the police, it appeared as a threat to wage war, though the Judicial Magistrate refused remand. 'Laugh at what?' is a serious question, the Judge said, using the 'holy cow' as a metaphor, which varies from person to person, region to region. Being funny is one thing, the Judge righty states, and poking fun at another is different altogether. Those who have been at the receiving end for their attempt at humour can draw strength from the ruling, but then, a creative process facing combative opposition because of its very nature is anything but funny.

126. What is the central idea in the passage as conveyed by the author?

    A. People need to be sensitive towards others' sensibilities.
    B. Humour is often used as a garb to offend others.
    C. There is an unwelcome decrease in people's sense of humour.
    D. Judiciary should use humour to make judgments understandable to laypersons.

127. According to the given passage, which of the following statements is true?

    A. Social media often popularised insensitive and offensive posts.
    B. It should be a right of every person to poke fun at others.
    C. Creative expressions are bound to be offensive to some persons.
    D. Every humorous expression should be understood reasonably and rationally.

128. According to the given passage, which of the following statements is not true?

    A. Each expression should be understood according to its context.
    B. The word 'shooting' used in a sentence is indicative of waging war.
    C. Legal process can be abused if the authorities act on their irrational impulses.
    D. The expression 'holy cow' bears different meanings for different people.

129. As per the passage, which of the following approaches can reduce the increasing 'idiocy and absurdity' in responding to expressions made in jest?

    A. Apologising upon hurting another person's sentiments.
    B. Avoiding the use of controversial words and expressions.
    C. Using humour as a means to mitigate conflict.
    D. Understanding the difference between being funny and poking fun at another person.

130. *"Those who have been at the receiving end for their attempt at humour can draw strength from the ruling, but then, a creative process facing combative opposition because of its very nature is anything but funny."*

Which of the following conclusions can be drawn from the above statement?

    A. Creativity and conflict go hand-in-hand.
    B. Creative freedom should not be curbed unreasonably.
    C. Creative expressions are strengthened due to challenges faced by their authors.
    D. Creativity often leads to conflict.

XXVII. Two recent developments have brought India's reliance on fossil fuel into sharp focus. The Russia-Ukraine conflict and the consequent surge in crude oil prices roiled the economy. Separately, the most recent IPCC report on climate highlighted the energy sector's large contribution to global warming. Both these developments need to be located in the context of India's pledge to get to net zero carbon emissions by 2070. Meeting this pledge requires an overhaul of both the logistics and electricity sectors to reduce reliance on fossil fuels. Transitioning to renewables in energy is an important part of the solution. Within renewables, solar energy has been lavished with policy support. However, it won't be enough to meet the targets. Anil Kakodkar, former chairman of Atomic Energy Commission, had written that India can't meet its net-zero commitment without nuclear power. He's right. It's an area where India was off to an early start, developed relatively high indigenous capabilities in relation to other sectors, but subsequently let the ball drop. Today, nuclear power contributes a mere 3% of the total electricity generated, and has a capacity of 6780 MW. After the early euphoria of the India-United States civil nuclear deal, progress has been disappointing. The

deal did open the pathway to a stable supply of uranium ore from Kazakhstan and Canada. However, the design of the subsequent bill on civil liability for nuclear damage killed the

prospect of participation of Western firms. India's main partner today is Russia, which side stepped the bill through inter-government agreements.

131. What is the central idea in the passage as conveyed by the author?

    A. India needs to increase use of nuclear power.
    B. India needs to increase production of fossil fuels.
    C. India needs to enter into multilateral agreements addressing use of nuclear power.
    D. Nuclear energy is a renewable source of power.

132. According to the author, which of the following measures will not help India achieve its pledge of net zero carbon emissions by 2070?

    A. Logistical changes
    B. Changes in electricity sector
    C. Reduction in use of solar power
    D. Increase in use of nuclear power

133. According to the author, which of the following is not the effect of India's reliance on fossil fuels?

    A. Global warming
    B. Increase in crude oil prices
    C. Relations with Middle East
    D. Less reliance on renewable sources of power

134. According to the author, which of the following is the effect of the India-United States civil nuclear deal?

    A. Export-Import target with United States
    B. Removal of bottlenecks for self-reliance in power generation
    C. Nuclear Defence Pact with Kazakhstan
    D. Self-reliance in Solar Power

135. According to the author, Western firms lost the opportunity of doing business in the

nuclear production in India because:

A.  They had to pay hefty penalties for delay in supply
B.  They do not find nuclear power profitable
C.  They do not agree with India's place of nuclear plants
D.  They failed to circumvent internal laws by other bilateral instruments

**Quantitative Techniques**

Text        Box:        Quantitative
Techniques

XXVIII.  As per a survey conducted in a college out of total students enrolled i.e., 3,000 in 2020-21, 1,700 were girls and 1,300 were boys. Data regarding students opting for various streams viz., Non-Medical, Medical, Commerce, Arts and Fine Arts showed that 25% of the enrolled students opted non-medical and the percentage of girls in Non-Medical was 30% of the total number of girls; 15% of the total students opted for Medical and the percentage of girls who opted Medical was 18% of the total number of girls; 25% of the total students opted Arts but the percentage of girls who opted for Arts was 15% of the total number of girls; 16% of the total students opted Commerce and the percentage of girls who opted Commerce was 17% of the total number of girls, and; 19% of the total students opted Fine Arts and the percentage of girls who opted Fine Arts was 20% of the total number of girls.

136.  How many girls have opted Non-Medical?

(A) 440 (B) 365 (C) 530 (D) 510

137.  Girls have outnumbered boys in Fine Arts. How many girls in Fine Arts are more than the boys, as a percentage of total number of boys in Fine Arts?

(A) 49.62% (B) 47.82% (C) 51.23% (D) 50.89%

138.  Which of the following courses have been opted by maximum number of boys?

A.  Non-Medical (B) Arts

(C) Fine Arts (D) Commerce

139.  Which of the following courses have been opted by minimum number of boys?

A.  Medical (B) Fine Arts

(C) Commerce (D) Non-Medical

140.  What is the ratio among boys and girls for Non-Medical?

(A) 3 : 17 (B) 17 : 8 (C) 8 : 17 (D) 17 : 3

XXIX.  An Indian company, having its registered office at Gurugram, is engaged in manufacturing of consumer goods at Noida. The goods manufactured by the company are sold in Indian market and exported to Europe. Company produces five products namely 'P','Q','R','S' and 'T'. Total production of the company for the financial year 2021-22 is 3,000 tonnes and the turnover of the company is ` 50 million. An analysis of the production and net revenue generation shows that production of product 'P' is 21% of the total production and 18% of the turnover is attributable to product 'P'; production of 'Q' is 16% of the total production and 17% of the turnover is attributable to 'Q'; 'R' accounts for 18% of the total production and 20% of the turnover; 'S' accounts for 20% of the total production and 25% of the turnover, and; 'T' accounts for 25% of total production and 20% of turnover.

141. What is the percentage of profit earned from sale of 'R', if the expenditure incurred

on production of 'R' is ` 15,000/- per tonne?
(A) 20% (B) 23.46%
(C) 26.55% (D) 25%

142. Which product has the highest selling price per tonne?

A. Q (B) R (C) S (D) T

143. How much loss is incurred to company, if the expenditure on production of 'T' was

` 20,000 per tonne?

A. 5 million (B) 10 million (C) 4 million (D) 7 million

144. What percentage of turnover of 'R' has to turnover of 'T'?

(A) 100% (B) 75% (C) 50% (D) 60%

145. What is the average selling price per tonne of all products taken together? (A) ` 17,488 (B) ` 17,667 (C) ` 18,667 (D) ` 16,667

XXX. In an organization, the total number of employees working in various Departments viz. IT, Marketing, Purchase, HR, Accounts and Production are 4,500. The information regarding department wise percentage of employees was collected and also record about gender ratio of employees was prepared. 18 percent of total number of employees work in IT department and ratio of males to females in IT department is 2 : 1. In Marketing, ratio of males to females is 2 : 3 and number of employees engaged in marketing is 20% of the total employment. 12% of the total numbers of workers are running the HR department and the ratio of males to females in this department is 5 : 1. The fraction of male to females in production department is 3 : 2 and total number of persons employed in this department is 15% of the total workforce. The number of persons occupied in purchase and accounts department is 24% and 11% respectively of the total number of workers. Gender Ratio (Ratio of males to females) in Purchase department is 1 : 1 and in Accounts is 1 : 2.

146. How many females are employed in Purchase department?

(A) 450 (B) 540 (C) 495 (D) 595

147. How many employees are working in IT and Accounts departments together? (A) 1,702 (B) 1,646 (C) 1,766 (D) 1,305

148. What is the ratio of total number of males to total number of females working in all the departments put together?

(A) 63 : 41 (B) 19 : 27 (C) 41 : 34 (D) 34 : 41

149. Number of females in Marketing Department forms what percentage of the total number of employees in the organization?

(A) 8% (B) 7% (C) 12% (D) 10%

150. What is the ratio of number of males in Marketing Department to the number of males in HR department?

(A) 4 : 5 (B) 5 : 4 (C) 7 : 3 (D) 6 : 7

**SPACE FOR ROUGH WORK**

# ANSWER KEY TO UG QUESTION PAPER 2022

## CLAT 2022
## FINAL ANSWER KEY – U.G.

| Ques No. | Correct Answer | Ques No. | Correct Answer | Ques No. | Correct Answer | Ques No. | Correct Answer |
|---|---|---|---|---|---|---|---|
| 1 | B | 41 | D | 81 | C | 121 | B |
| 2 | C | 42 | A | 82 | D | 122 | A |
| 3 | D | 43 | D | 83 | B | 123 | D |
| 4 | C | 44 | C | 84 | D | 124 | D |
| 5 | A | 45 | B | 85 | A | 125 | C |
| 6 | D | 46 | C | 86 | C | 126 | C |
| 7 | C | 47 | A | 87 | C | 127 | D |
| 8 | B | 48 | B | 88 | A | 128 | B |
| 9 | B | 49 | A | 89 | D | 129 | D |
| 10 | A | 50 | D | 90 | C | 130 | B |
| 11 | D | 51 | B | 91 | D | 131 | A |
| 12 | A | 52 | C | 92 | B | 132 | C |
| 13 | B | 53 | C | 93 | C | 133 | C |
| 14 | D | 54 | D | 94 | C | 134 | B |
| 15 | C | 55 | A | 95 | D | 135 | D |
| 16 | C | 56 | D | 96 | A | 136 | D |
| 17 | D | 57 | B | 97 | C | 137 | B |
| 18 | B | 58 | A | 98 | A | 138 | B |
| 19 | A | 59 | C | 99 | A | 139 | A |
| 20 | D | 60 | D | 100 | C | 140 | C |
| 21 | C | 61 | A | 101 | A | 141 | B |
| 22 | D | 62 | C | 102 | D | 142 | C |
| 23 | B | 63 | D | 103 | D | 143 | A |
| 24 | C | 64 | A | 104 | A | 144 | A |
| 25 | C | 65 | B | 105 | C | 145 | D |
| 26 | B | 66 | A | 106 | A | 146 | B |
| 27 | D | 67 | B | 107 | C | 147 | D |
| 28 | A | 68 | C | 108 | A | 148 | C |
| 29 | A | 69 | A | 109 | A | 149 | C |
| 30 | D | 70 | D | 110 | C | 150 | A |
| 31 | B | 71 | B | 111 | A |  |  |
| 32 | C | 72 | B | 112 | C |  |  |
| 33 | D | 73 | C | 113 | D |  |  |
| 34 | C | 74 | C | 114 | A |  |  |
| 35 | A | 75 | A | 115 | C |  |  |
| 36 | D | 76 | B | 116 | B |  |  |
| 37 | C | 77 | B | 117 | A |  |  |
| 38 | C | 78 | A | 118 | A |  |  |
| 39 | A | 79 | D | 119 | C |  |  |
| 40 | D | 80 | D | 120 | C |  |  |

Enter Caption

# CHAPTER SEVEN

# PG QUESTION PAPER 2022

**PG 2022**

**CONSORTIUM OF NATIONAL LAW UNIVERSITIES COMMON LAW ADMISSION TEST-2022**

## LL.M. Programme

### INSTRUCTIONS TO CANDIDATES

*(This Booklet contains 36 pages of Question Paper including 3 blank pages for rough work.)*
**Duration of Test : 2 Hours (120 Minutes) Maximum Marks : 120**

1. Separate carbonised Optical Mark Reader (OMR) Response Sheet is supplied along with this Question Booklet and the carbon copy has to be detached and taken by the candidates.
2. In case of any discrepancy in the question booklet (QB), please request the Invigilator for replacement of a fresh packet of QB with OMR. Do not use the previous OMR Response Sheet for a fresh booklet so obtained.
3. Candidates will not be given a second blank OMR Response Sheet under any circumstance. Hence, OMR Response Sheet shall be handled carefully.
4. Answer all questions. No clarification can be sought on the Question Paper.
5. Possession of Electronic Devices in any form is Strictly prohibited in the Examination Hall.
6. The use of any unfair means by any candidate shall result in the cancellation of his/her examination.
7. Impersonation is an offense and the candidate, apart from disqualification, will be liable to be prosecuted.
8. The Test Paper for Post Graduate (LL.M.) Programme is for 120 marks containing 120 Multiple Choice Questions.
9. There will be Negative marking for multiple choice objective type questions. **0.25 marks** will be deducted for every wrong answer or where candidates have marked more than one response.

10. Use **BLACK/BLUE BALL POINT PEN** only for writing the Roll No. and other details on OMR Response Sheet.
11. Use **BLACK/BLUE BALL POINT PEN** for shading the circles. Indicate only **the most appropriate answer** by shading from the options provided. The answer circle should be shaded completely without leaving any space.
12. As the responses cannot be modified/corrected on the OMR Response Sheet, candidates have to take necessary precautions before marking the appropriate circle.
13. The candidate should retain the Admit Card duly Signed by the Invigilator, as the same has to be produced at the time of Admission.
14. Handle the OMR Response Sheet with care. Do not fold.
15. Ensure that Invigilator puts his/her signature in the space provided on the OMR Response Sheet. Candidate should sign in the space provided on the OMR Response Sheet.
16. The candidate should write Question Paper Booklet No., and OMR Response Sheet No., and sign in the space/column provided in the attendance sheet.
17. Return the ORIGINAL Page of OMR Response Sheet to the Invigilator after the Examination.

18. The candidate shall not write anything on the OMR Response Sheet other than the details required and in the spaces provided for.

**M**

---

I.  Both lawmen and laymen often ask, '*What is the law applicable to a given set of facts?*' The answers to this question differ depending upon the specific jurisdiction to which the given set of facts is linked. Contrary to this, scholars and students of jurisprudence are likely to ask the general question, viz 'What is Law?'. This question on the philosophy and nature of law supposes that law is a distinctive social-political phenomenon with universal characteristics that can be perceived through philosophical analysis. In such a study, the assumption is that law possesses some universal characteristics.

An analysis of the philosophy of law can be done for different reasons. Apart from a purely intellectual interest in understanding this complex phenomenon known as law, scholars also study the same as a normative social practice that purports to guide human behaviour, giving rise to reasons for action. The primary challenge of the branch of scholarship known as jurisprudence is based on this 'normative, reason-giving aspect of law'. At the same time, we must understand that law is not the only normative realm in any given society. It is one of the many normative standards such as morality, religion, customs and usages, etiquette, self-regulatory standards within a family or corporation etc. So, it is also essential that we study law on the differences and similarities of the same with these normative standards.

While discerning these connections and contradictions, legal theories often study the content of the norm apart from giving importance to the source. Generally, theoretical studies on the content such as natural lawyers emphasize values such as fairness, justice, liberty etc., as qualifications for the norms to be called laws. They have argued that laws must be in tune with certain principles of inner morality, such as that laws be general, public, prospective, coherent, clear, stable, and practicable are indispensable to law-making. Whereas theories that give prominence to the sources of the norm, such as enactment/command by political institution/authority, do not always emphasize on the content.

Such philosophical analysis of law comprises both explanatory and justificatory aspects. While the explanatory aspect consists of explaining how laws can give rise to reasons and what kinds of reasons are involved. One example of this would be Dworkin's classification of law as concepts, principles and rules. The aspect of justification concerns whether people ought to comply with the law's demands. In other words, it is the attempt to explain the moral legitimacy of law and the subjects' reasons for complying with it.

1.  Validity of law resides in the political sovereignty of the maker of that law refers to:

    A.  Legal Positivism (B) Natural Law

(C) Historical School (D) Sociological School

2.  A norm cannot become legally valid unless its content is fair and just in accordance to:

    A.  Legal Positivism (B) Natural Law

(C) Historical School (D) Sociological School

3.  "*The falsehood of legal positivism resides in envisaging that the law consists of only rules. However, this is a serious mistake since legal principles partly determine the law in addition to rules. The distinction between rules*

*and principles is a logical one. Rules apply in an 'all or nothing fashion.' If the rule applies to the circumstances, it determines a particular legal outcome. If it does not apply, it is simply irrelevant to the outcome.....*" according to:

A.  Ronald Dworkin, Taking Rights Seriously,1977
B.  John Finnis, Natural Law and Natural Rights, 1980.
C.  H.L.A.Hart, The Concept of Law, 1961.
D.  Raz, Joseph, Legal Principles and the Limits of Law, 1972.

4.  Principles requiring that laws be general, public, prospective, coherent, clear, stable, and practicable are indispensable to law-making correspond to:

A.  Inner Morality (B) Method of logic

(C) Legitimacy and Transparency in law making (D) Democratic law making

5.  'I mean simply that history, in illuminating the past, illuminates the present, and in illuminating the present, illuminates the future' opined by:

A.  Roscoe Pound (B) Benjamin Cardozo

(C) Duguit (D) Auguste Comte

6.  'The life of the law has not been logic: it has been experience' is stated by:

A.  Holmes (B) Dworkin

(C) Cardozo (D) Amartya Sen

II.  A thought-provoking book titled 'The Morality of Law' by Lon L. Fuller on moral philosophy insists on a distinction between 'morality of aspiration' and 'morality of duty'. From the view of the morality of aspiration, the human conduct does not bear on mandatory rules but on conceptions of the 'Good Life', of 'what beseems a human being functioning at his best to human capacities'. Because no law can compel a man to live up to the excellence of which he is capable. But for workable standards of judgment, the morality of duty lays down the

basic rules without which an ordered society directed towards certain specific goals must fail of its mark. Because the duty ties it very closely to what is 'rationally discoverable' and 'objective', as contrasted with the morality of aspiration based on subjectivism. However, moralists may differ as to what range of conduct should fall within the respective spheres of duty and the morality of aspirations. *"When we are passing a judgment of moral duty, it seems absurd to say that such a duty can in some way flow directly from knowledge of a situation of fact."* As due to the fact that before we conclude 'that a duty ought to exist', however well we may understand the facts, by the close connection between understanding a person's ideals, approval and disapproval. Does this mean that duties are rationally discoverable, and a matter of choice, even if not of 'ineffable preference'? Presumably not, since when we pass a moral judgment of duty 'ought' to exist. It is necessary to distinguish between the accepted morality of a social group and the personal morality of individuals. 'Duty' may appear in all of these, but the satisfaction is very often a matter of degree varying from situation to situation. The rule of a morality of duty is necessary for social living. The morality of aspiration provides a general idea of the perfection we ought to acquire it. If we consider the whole range of moral issues, we may imagine a yardstick which begins at the bottom with the most obvious demands of social living and extends upward to the highest reaches of human aspirations. Somewhere along this scale an invisible pointer marks the dividing line where the pressure of duty leaves off and the challenge of excellence begins. The whole field of moral argument is an undeclared war over the location of this pointer. Whom we regard as being moralistic are always trying to inch the pointer upward so as to expand the area of duty and they bludgeon us into a belief that we are duty bound to embrace this pattern of human conduct, instead of making us realize a pattern of life they consider worthy of human nature.

7.  Which of the following statements regarding the 'morality of aspiration' is untrue?

A.  The morality of aspiration is based on inevitable rules for ordered social living.
B.  The morality of aspiration impulses towards the perfection and excellence.
C.  The law cannot regulate the morality of aspiration because it is subjective in nature.
D.  The law cannot compel a man to adhere to the best of his human capabilities.

8.  The rules for morality of duty command:

A.  To conduct best to human capacity. (B) To conduct necessary for self-survival.

(C) To conduct equally as others' conduct. (D) To conduct necessary for social living.

9.  Consider the statements:

I.  The moralistic philosophy always strives to encroach into the area of morality of aspiration to bring it as duty for the social living.
II.  The moralistic philosophers compel us to embrace the pattern of human conduct, instead of making us realize a pattern of life that is worthy of human nature.

Choose the correct answer from the code given below.
(A) Both (I) and (II) are true. (B) Both (I) and (II) are untrue.
(C) (I) is true and (II) is untrue. (D) (II) is true and (I) is untrue.

10.  Which of the following element is not required for the formation of decision regarding a moral duty?

A.  Rationality (B) Objectivity

(C) Subjectivity (D) Knowledge regarding the circumstances

11.  The concept of duty as characterised by Lon L. Fuller seems

A.  Dynamic (B) Static (C) Personal (D) Fictional

12.  Which of the following statements is not true?

A.  'Morality of duty' is non-obligatory.
B.  'Morality of duty' is obligatory.
C.  Rules of 'morality of aspiration' are a challenge to human conduct.
D.  Human excellence is the end of 'morality of aspiration'.

III. The present system of appointments as envisaged by the Constitution and as elucidated in the Collegium system makes it clear that the first step is a recommendation from Collegium of four senior-most judges and presided over by the Chief Justice. This process in turn requires wide consultation by the Chief Justice of the High Court to identify the requisite talent, so as to make the recommendations. Contrary to some portrayed beliefs as if this is an extremely subjective system, every Chief Justice is actually required to solicit names from different sources whether it be sitting judges, retired judges, or prominent members of the Bar. It is from this pool of talent that he selects, after a discussion in the collegium, the most suitable candidates. It is thus of utmost importance that the flow of recommendations continues for the appointment process to work successfully. The current situation of vacancies, especially in some of the larger courts with very few recommendations in the pipeline seems to be the genesis of this problem. The data placed before us, as drawn from the National Judicial Data Grid (NJDG) shows that five (5) High Courts alone are responsible for 54% of the pendency of over 57,51,312 cases i.e., the High Courts of Allahabad, Punjab & Haryana, Madras, Bombay, and Rajasthan. The Madras High Court has among the highest arrears in the country of 5.8 lakh cases despite having fewer vacancies than most other High Courts (i.e., 7%). This does not take away from the requirement of appointing ad hoc Judges but supports the view that even if the existing vacancies are few, a situation may arise requiring the expertise of experienced Judges to be appointed as *ad hoc* Judges.

13. The above excerpt has been taken from which of the following judgments, where the Supreme Court of India sought to activate a dormant provision of the Constitution of India for the appointment of *ad hoc* Judges to deal with the unprecedented backlog of cases pending before the High Courts ?

   A. Devendra Kumar Saxena v. Central Bureau of Investigation (CBI), 2021 SCC OnLine SC 330.
   B. M.K. Ranjitsinh v. Union of India, 2021 SCC OnLine SC 326.
   C. Lok Prahari through its General Secretary S.N. Shukla, IAS (Retd.) v. Union of India, 2021 SCC OnLine SC 333.
   D. Justice V. Eswaraiah (Retd.) v. Union of India, 2021 SCC OnLine SC 310.

14. Which of the following dormant provision of the Constitution of India has been invoked by the Supreme Court of India for the appointment of *ad hoc* Judges to deal with the backlog of cases before the High Courts?

   A. Article 224A (B) Article 217

(C) Article 224 (D) Article 217A

15. In *Supreme Court Advocates on Record Association v. Union of India,* (2016) 5 SCC 1, the Supreme Court of India, by a majority, restored the collegium system of appointment of judges by holding that the National Judicial Appointments Commission Act, 2014 is *ultra vires* the Constitution of India.

(A) 3:2 (B) 4:1 (C) 6:1 (D) 4:3

16. In which of the following cases the Supreme Court of India observed that for appointment of a retired Judge as an *adhoc* judge, the consent of such retired Judge is a pre-requisite for his/her appointment as an *ad hoc* judge?

   A. Ashok Tanwar v. State of Himachal Pradesh, (2005) 2 SCC 104.
   B. Supreme Court Advocates on Record Association v. Union of India, (2016) 5 SCC 1.
   C. Union of India v. Sankal Chand and Himatlal Sheth, (1977) 4 SCC 193.
   D. Krishan Gopal v. Shri Prakash Chandra, (1974) 1 SCC 128.

17.  In which of the following reports the Law Commission of India advocated for appointment of retired judges as *ad-hoc* judges in the interest of clearing backlogs of cases in the High Courts?

A.  One Hundred Eighty Eighth Report on proposals for Constitution of Hi-Tech Fast-Track Commercial Divisions in High Courts (2003).
B.  Fourteenth Report on Reforms in Judicial Administration (1958).
C.  One Twentieth Report on Manpower Planning in Judiciary: A Blueprint (1987).
D.  One Hundred Eighteenth Report on Method of Appointments to Subordinate Courts/ Subordinate Judiciary (1986).

18.  Which of the following statements is true regarding the origin of the Collegium system for appointment of judges?

A.  Article 124A of the Constitution of India provides for the establishment of the collegium system.
B.  The Judicial Appointments (Collegium System) Act, 1999 provides for the establishment of the collegium system.
C.  The Constitution of India does not provide for the establishment of the collegium system.
D.  The National Judicial Appointments Commission supplements the collegium system for appointment of judges.

IV.  The Supreme Court of India observed that, while appreciating the existence of the right to peaceful protest against a legislation ........, we have to make it unequivocally clear that public ways and public spaces cannot be occupied in such a manner and that too indefinitely. Democracy and dissent go hand in hand, but then the demonstrations expressing dissent must be in designated places alone. The present case was not even one of protests taking place in an undesignated area but was a blockage of a public way which caused grave inconvenience to commuters. We cannot accept the plea of the applicants that an indeterminable number of people can assemble whenever they choose to protest.

19.  Which of the following judgments relating to right to peaceful protest has the above excerpt been taken from?

A.  M.C. Mehta v. Union of India, 2020 SCC OnLine SC 648.
B.  Association for Democratic Reforms v. Union of India, 2021 SCC OnLine SC 266.
C.  Anuradha Bhasin v. Union of India, (2020) 3 SCC 637.
D.  Amit Sahni v. Commissioner of Police, (2020) 10 SCC 439.

20.  Which of the following judgments is not related to right to assemble as enshrined under the Constitution of India?

A.  Mazdoor Kisan Shakti Sangathan v. Union of India, (2018) 17 SCC 324.
B.  Sampurna Behura v. Union of India, (2018) 4 SCC 433.
C.  Bimal Gurung v. Union of India, (2018) 15 SCC 480.
D.  Anita Thakur v. State of Jammu and Kashmir, (2016) 15 SCC 525.

21.  As per the judgment of *In Re Ramlila Maidan Incident*, (2012) 5 SCC 1, which of the following statement is not correct?

A.  Right to sleep is not a part of Article 21 of the Constitution of India.
B.  An individual is entitled to sleep as comfortably and as freely as he breathes.

C. Sleep, is a fundamental and basic requirement without which the existence of life would be in peril.

D. State's compelling interest in regulation of subject was discussed in this case.

22. Which of the following statement is not correct in relation to right to assemble under the Constitution of India?

A. The assembly should be peaceful.

B. Reasonable restrictions stated under Article 19 for right to assemble are sovereignty and integrity of India or public order, morality.

C. The assembly should be without arms.

D. Reasonable restrictions on right to assemble are provided in Article 19(3) of the Constitution of India.

23. The rule prohibiting demonstrations by government servants was discussed in which of the following judgments?

A. Union of India v. Naveen Jindal, (2004) 2 SCC 510.

B. Ram Bahadur Rai v. State of Bihar, AIR 1975 SC 223.

C. Kameshwar Prasad v. State of Bihar, AIR 1962 SC 1166.

D. Bennett Coleman & Co. v. Union of India, AIR 1973 SC 106.

24. Which of the following judges of the Supreme Court of India were part of the Bench in the judgment as given in the excerpt?

A. Sanjay Kishan Kaul, Aniruddha Bose and Indira Banerjee, JJ.

B. Aniruddha Bose and Krishna Murari, JJ.

C. Sanjay Kishan Kaul, Aniruddha Bose and Krishna Murari, JJ.

D. Sanjay Kishan Kaul and Krishna Murari, JJ.

V. The Supreme Court of India has held that the rationale of granting maintenance from the date of application finds its roots in the object of enacting maintenance legislations, so as to enable the wife to overcome the financial crunch which occurs on separation from the husband. Financial constraints of a dependant spouse hamper their capacity to be effectively represented before the Court. Enforcement of the order of maintenance is the most challenging issue, which is encountered by the applicants. If maintenance is not paid in a timely manner, it defeats the very object of the social welfare legislation. Execution petitions usually remain pending for months, if not years, which completely nullifies the object of the law.

25. Based on the given excerpt from the judgment, which of the following judgments is related to enforcement of orders of maintenance and successive claims by parties in matrimonial proceedings?

A. Smriti Madan Kansagra v. Perry Kansagra, 2020 SCC OnLine SC 1003.

B. Rajnesh v. Neha, (2021) 2 SCC 324.

C. Roshina T. v. Abdul Azeez K.T., (2019) 2 SCC 329.

D. Manju Saxena v. Union of India, (2019) 2 SCC 628.

26. Which of the following reliefs does the Hindu Marriage Act, 1955 provide?

A. Maintenance *Pendente lite*, expenses of proceedings, permanent alimony and maintenance.

B. Expenses of proceedings, permanent alimony and maintenance.

C. Maintenance *Pendente lite*, permanent alimony and maintenance.

D.  Maintenance *Pendente lite*, expenses of proceedings, permanent alimony.

27.  Which of the following statutes does not contain provisions relating to maintenance?

A.  The Parsi Marriage and Divorce Act, 1936.
B.  The Special Marriage Act, 1954.
C.  The Prohibition of Child Marriage Act, 2006.
D.  The Muslim Women (Protection of Rights on Marriage) Act, 2019.

28.  Which of the following is not a direction given by Supreme Court of India in the judgement relating to orders of maintenance and successive claims by parties in matrimonial proceedings?

A.  Where successive claims for maintenance are made by a party under different statutes, the Court would consider an adjustment or setoff of the amount awarded in previous proceedings.
B.  If the order passed in the previous proceeding/s requires any modification or variation,

it would be required to be done in the same proceeding.

C.  It is not mandatory for the applicant to disclose the previous proceeding and the orders passed therein, in the subsequent proceeding.
D.  The affidavit of disclosure of assets and liabilities as applicable, shall be filed by both parties in all maintenance proceedings, including pending proceedings before any other court, as the case may be.

29.  Which of the following is not correct as per Section 125 of the Code of Criminal Procedure, 1973?

A.  It provides for maintenance to wife/wives, illegitimate and legitimate children and parents.
B.  A wife shall not be entitled to receive maintenance as per this provision from her husband if she is living in adultery, or if, without any sufficient reason, she refuses to live with her husband, or if they are living separately by mutual consent.
C.  A magistrate has been given wide powers under this provision.
D.  As per the explanation under this provision, wife does not include a woman who has been divorced by, or has obtained a divorce from, her husband but includes a woman who has remarried.

30.  Which of the following is correct about the Hindu Adoptions and Maintenance Act, 1956?

A.  It is a special legislation which was enacted to provide for maintenance to wife during the subsistence of the marriage.
B.  The Supreme Court of India considered the interplay between the claim for maintenance under the Hindu Marriage Act, 1955 and Hindu Adoptions and Maintenance Act, 1956 in *Chand Dhawan v. Jawaharlal Dhawan*, (1993) 3 SCC 406.
C.  Section 18 of the Act provides that a Hindu wife shall be entitled to be maintained by her husband during her lifetime.
D.  As per Section 18 of the Act, a Hindu wife is not entitled to make a claim for a separate residence from her husband, without forfeiting her right to maintenance.

VI.  The Supreme Court of India has held that the nature of inquiry before the Family Court is, indeed, adjudicatory. It is obliged to resolve the rival claims of the parties and while doing so, it must adhere to the norms prescribed by the statute in that regard and also the foundational principle of fairness of procedure and natural justice. These provisions plainly reveal that the Family Court is expected to follow procedure known to law, which means insist for a formal pleading to be filed by both sides, then frame the issues for determination, record the evidence of the parties to prove the facts asserted by the concerned party and only thereafter, to enter upon determination and render decision thereon by recording the reasons for such decision. For doing this, the Family Court is expected to give notice to the respective parties and provide them sufficient time and opportunity to present their claim in the form of pleadings and evidence before determination of the dispute.

31. Which of the following is not correct about the Family Courts Act, 1984?

    A. The Act intends to promote conciliation and secure speedy settlement of disputes.
    B. The appointment of counsellors in family courts is determined by the State Government in consultation with the High Court.
    C. The duty of the Family Court is to arrive at a settlement between the parties where it is possible and consistent with the nature and circumstances of the case.
    D. A person can be appointed as a judge of the Family Court after the attainment of sixty-two years of age.

32. Based on the given excerpt, which of the following judgments is related to the working of Family Courts?

    A. Sanjiv Prakash v. Seema Kukreja, 2021 SCC OnLine SC 282.
    B. Khushi Ram v. Nawal Singh, 2021 SCC OnLine SC 128.
    C. Aman Lohia v. Kiran Lohia, 2021 SCC OnLine SC 224.
    D. Gurmeet Pal Singh v. State of Punjab,(2018) 7 SCC 260.

33. Based on the given excerpt, which of the following was held by the Supreme Court of India in relation to the Family Courts?

    A. Non-compliance of the prescribed mandatory procedure and infraction of principles of natural justice is not a technical irregularity which can be overlooked by family courts.
    B. In divorce proceedings, it is the duty of family courts to mandatorily conduct mediation between the parties.
    C. Non-compliance of the prescribed mandatory procedure and infraction of principles of natural justice is a technical irregularity which can be overlooked by family courts.
    D. Family Courts ought not to examine matters after giving due opportunity to both sides on their own merits and in accordance with law.

34. The Family Court must adhere to the norms prescribed by the statute with regard to the adjudication of matrimonial disputes, and also to the:

    A. Convenience of the court.
    B. Fair procedure and natural justice.
    C. International conventions.
    D. Convenience of the parties.

35. Which of the following is not correct about the nature of proceedings conducted in the Family Court?

    A. The proceedings must always be held in camera.
    B. The Act provides that if the Family Court considers it necessary in the interest of justice, it may seek the assistance of a legal expert as *amicus curiae*.

    C.  The proceedings may be held in camera depending on the desire of court and the party concerned.

    D.  Family Court may secure the services of a medical expert if required.

36.  The Family Courts Act, 1984 does not apply to which of the following matters?

    A.  Divorce under Hindu Law.

    B.  *Nikah* as per Muslim Personal Law.

    C.  Marriage under Special Marriage Act, 1954.

    D.  Adoption under Hindu Law.

VII.  The Supreme Court of India, in *South East Asia Marine Engineering & Constructions Ltd. (SEAMEC LTD.) v. Oil India Ltd.,*(2020) 5 SCC 164, noted that, under the Indian contract law, the consequences of a force majeure event are provided for under Section 56 of the Indian Contract Act, 1872 which deals with a contract to do an Act which, after the contract is made, becomes impossible, or, by reason of some event which the promisor could not prevent, unlawful, becomes void when the Act becomes impossible or unlawful. When the parties have not provided for what would take place when an event which renders the performance of the contract impossible, then Section 56 applies. When the Act contracted for becomes impossible, then under Section 56, the parties are exempted from further performance and the contract becomes void. The Court has further held that in Section 56, the word 'impossible' is to be

taken in its practical and not literal sense. It must be borne in mind, however, that Section 56 lays down a rule of positive law and does not leave the matter to be determined according to the intention of the parties. However, there is no doubt that the parties may instead choose the consequences that would flow on the happening of an uncertain future event, under Section 32 of the Indian Contract Act, 1872.

37.  Mr. X agrees with Mr. Y to discover by magic, a treasure supposed to be buried within certain limits at an unknown spot. Mr. X found the treasure subsequently.Consider the given facts and answer which of the following statement is correct?

    A.  Law can regard a promise to do something obviously impossible as significant.

    B.  Such promises are based on legal considerations.

    C.  Law cannot regard a promise to do something obviously impossible to be of any value.

    D.  The agreement is valid and binding.

38.  Which of the following is correct regarding the Doctrine of Frustration of Contract?

    A.  It leaves the contract to be determined in accordance with the intention of the parties.

    B.  It is based on the subsequent impossibility of the agreement which is frustrated by the intrusion or occurrence of an unexpected event which is within the contemplation by the parties.

    C.  It does not necessarily make the contract impossible of performance.

    D.  In case of change of circumstances which is so fundamental as to be regarded by law as striking at the root of the contract, court cannot pronounce the contract to be frustrated.

39.  Consider the meaning of 'Impossibility' from the given excerpt: *IndecidingcasesinIndia, the only doctrine that we have to go by is that of supervening impossibility or illegality as laid down in Section 56 of the Contract Act 1872, taking the word 'impossible' in its practical and not literal sense.* Which of the following is correct regarding the nature of impossibility in such contracts?

A. The performance of the act may not be literally impossible, but it may be impracticable from the point of view of the object.
B. The changed circumstances never make the performance of the contract impossible.
C. The performance of the act may not be literally impossible, but it may be practicable from the point of view of the object.
D. The parties are not absolved from the further performance of a contract if they do not promise to perform an impossibility.

40. Consider the given statement: *Law does not compel a person to do which he cannot possibly perform.* Which of the following legal maxims correctly expresses the meaning of the given statement?

A. *Res Ipsa Loquitur* (B) *Sub Silentio*

(C) *Actio Personalis Moritur Cum Persona* (D) *Impotentia Excusat Legem*

41. Which of the following will not make a contract frustrated even after a supervening impossibility ?

A. The contract is not absolute in terms and does not cover the impossibility.
B. The contract is absolute and covers the impossibility.
C. It cannot be reasonably foreseen by the parties at the time of formation of contract.
D. If the object of the contract becomes impracticable.

42. Which of the following is correct regarding considerations in deciding issues of frustration of contract ?

A. The Doctrine of Frustration will not be applicable to assist a party that does not

want to fulfil its obligations under the contract.

B. The defence of Doctrine of Frustration is not available to a person who for the reason of impossibility cannot perform the contract.
C. Few variations from the original contract will be a defence for the parties.
D. The intervening event must not be entirely impossible.

VIII. The constitutional validity of the West Bengal Housing Industry Regulation Act, 2017 (WB-HIRA) was challenged on the basis that both WB-HIRA and a Parliamentary enactment, namely, the Real Estate (Regulation and Development) Act, 2016 (RERA) are relatable to the legislative subjects contained in Entries 6 and 7 of List III (Concurrent List) of the Seventh Schedule of the Constitution of India. WB-HIRA has neither been reserved for nor has it received Presidential assent under Article 254(2) of the Constitution of India, which was necessary since it was going to occupy the same field as the RERA, a law which had been enacted by the Parliament. The State enactment contains certain provisions which are either: directly inconsistent with the corresponding provisions of the Central enactment; or a virtual replica of the Central enactment; and Parliament having legislated on a field covered by the Concurrent List, it is constitutionally impermissible for the State Legislature to enact a law over the same subject matter by setting up a parallel legislation. The analysis indicates repugnancy between WB-HIRA and RERA. Undoubtedly, as Article 254(1) postulates, the legislation enacted by the State legislature is void 'to the extent of the repugnancy'. There is, not only a direct conflict of certain provisions between the RERA and WB-HIRA, but there is also a failure of the State legislature to incorporate statutory safeguards in WB-HIRA, which have been introduced in the RERA for protecting the interest of the purchasers of real estate. For repugnancy under Article 254 of the Constitution, there is a twin requirement to be fulfilled: firstly, there has to be a 'repugnancy' between a Central and State Act; and secondly, the Presidential assent has to be held as being non-existent. The test for determining such repugnancy is indeed to find out the dominant intention of both the legislations and whether such dominant intentions of both the legislations are alike or different. A provision in one legislation in order to give effect to its dominant purpose may incidentally be on the same subject as covered by the provision of the other legislation, but such partial or incidental coverage of the same area in a different context and to achieve a different purpose does not attract the doctrine of repugnancy. In order to attract the doctrine of repugnancy, both the legislations must be substantially on the same subject. Hence, WB-HIRA is repugnant to the RERA, and is hence unconstitutional.

43. Which of the following is not an element of the twin requirement test to determine repugnancy under Article 254 of the Constitution of India?

   A.  Repugnancy between the Central Act and State Act within the Concurrent List.
   B.  State Act has been reserved for the consideration of the President.
   C.  State Act has received accent of the President.
   D.  Both (B) and (C).

44. Which of the following statements regarding Entry 7 of List III (Concurrent List) of Seventh Schedule of the Constitution of India is untrue ?

   A.  Contract relating to carriage of goods falls under Entry 7 of the Concurrent List.
   B.  Contract relating to agriculture land falls under Entry 7 of the Concurrent List.
   C.  Contract relating to agency falls under Entry 7 of the Concurrent List.
   D.  Contract relating to partnership falls under Entry 7 of the Concurrent List.

45. Where the State legislature enacts an Act on a subject vested to State legislature by the Constitution of India, if incidentally, the provisions of such a State Act operates on a subject which is exclusively vested to the Parliament, such incidental coverage of the same area shall attract the test of:

   A.  Repugnancy (B) Pith and substance

   (C) Colourable legislation (D) Superior legislation

46. The word 'assent' used in Article 254 (2) of the Constitution of India means:

   A.  A constitutional formality of obtaining consent of the President for promulgating a new Act.
   B.  An express agreement of mind to what is proposed by the State Legislature by enacting a new law on the same subject on which the Central law already exists.
   C.  An express agreement of mind to what is proposed by the State Legislature regarding repugnancy.
   D.  Both (B) and (C).

47. Article 254 (2) of the Constitution of India applies to the matters enumerated in:

   A.  The Union List (B) The State List

   (C) The Concurrent List (D) The Union List and the State List

48. In case of inconsistency between a law made by Parliament and law made by the Legislatures of State, the law made by the Legislature of the State shall:

   A. Completely be void.
   B. To the extent of the repugnancy, be void.
   C. At the discretion of the Parliament, be void.
   D. At the discretion of the Court, be void.

IX. In *Gautam Navlakha v. National Investigation Agency,* 2021 SCC OnLine SC 382, the court analysed the ambit of Article 22 of the Constitution of India and also the scope of the expression 'arrest' contained therein and also under the relevant provisions of the Code of Criminal Procedure, 1973 (CrPC). 'Arrest' may be classified into two categories, namely, the arrest under a warrant issued by a court and arrest without warrant. Section 57 of the Code of Criminal Procedure clearly directs that the investigation should be completed in the first instance within 24 hours; if not the arrested person should be brought before a Magistrate as provided under Section 167 of the Code of Criminal Procedure. Turning now to Article 22(1) and (2), we must ascertain whether its protection extends to both categories of arrests mentioned above, and, if not, then which one of them comes within its protection. There can be no matter of doubt that arrests without warrants issued by a court call for greater protection than do arrests under such warrants. The provision that the arrested person should within 24 hours be produced before the nearest Magistrate is particularly desirable in the case of arrest otherwise than under a warrant issued by the court, for it ensures the immediate application of a judicial mind to the legal authority of the person making the arrest and the regularity of the procedure adopted by him. In the case of arrest under a warrant issued by a court, the judicial mind had already been applied to the case when the warrant was issued and, therefore, there is less reason for making such production in that case a matter of a substantive fundamental right. The matter of 'House Arrest' was deliberated by the court as: *"There can be no quarrel with the proposition that a court cannot remand a person unless the court is authorised to do so by law. We are of the view, that in the facts of this case, the house arrest was not ordered purporting to be under Section 167. We observe that under Section 167 in appropriate cases it will be open to courts to order house arrest."*

49. Consider the following statements:

  I. The application of judicial mind is not necessary to issue a warrant by the court.
  II. The constitutional notion demands the application of judicial mind immediately after the arrest of person without a warrant.

Choose the correct answer from the code given below.
(A) Both (I) and (II) are true. (B) Both (I) and (II) are untrue.
(C) (I) is true and (II) is untrue. (D) (II) is true and (I) is untrue.

50. Section 57 of the Code of Criminal Procedure, 1973 applies to arrest warrant.

   A. With (B) Without

  (C) With or without (D) On execution of

———

51. The fundamental right under Article 22(2) of the Constitution of India regarding the duty of police to produce arrested person before the nearest Magistrate applies to:

    A.  Detenu who at the time of arrest is an enemy alien.
    B.  Arrest under any law providing for preventive detention.
    C.  Arrest under Section 41 of the Code of Criminal Procedure, 1973.
    D.  Arrest in execution of warrant issued by the court.

52. Section 167 of the Code of Criminal Procedure, 1973 empowers a Judicial Magistrate to authorise the detention of an accused in:

    A.  Police Custody.
    B.  Judicial Custody.
    C.  Both Police Custody and Judicial Custody.
    D.  Other than Police and Judicial Custody.

53. In *Gautam Navlakha v. National Investigation Agency*, 2021 SCC OnLine SC 382, the court did not consider the period of house arrest in calculating the period of custody for the purpose of filing the application for default bail because:

    A.  The order of house arrest was not purported to be under Section 167 the Code of Criminal Procedure, 1973.
    B.  The court is not authorized to order house arrest under Section 167 the Code of Criminal Procedure, 1973.
    C.  The order of house arrest was illegal.
    D.  The term 'house arrest' was not given anywhere under the Code of Criminal Procedure, 1973.

54. In *GautamNavlakhav.NationalInvestigationAgency*, 2021 SCC OnLine SC 382, the court has established that the order of the court to direct house arrest of the arrested person shall be:

    A.  Unconstitutional.
    B.  Within the competence of the court under Section 167 the Code of Criminal Procedure, 1973.
    C.  Beyond the competence of the court under Section 167 the Code of Criminal Procedure, 1973.
    D.  Discretionary.

X. Section 304-B (1) of the Indian Penal Code, 1860 (IPC) defines 'dowry death' of a woman. It provides that 'dowry death' is where death of a woman is caused by burning or bodily injuries or occurs otherwise than under normal circumstances, within seven years of marriage, and it is shown that soon before her death, she was subjected to cruelty or harassment by her husband or any relative of her husband, in connection with demand for dowry. Further, Section 304-B (2) of IPC provides punishment for the aforesaid offence. The Supreme Court of India summarized the law under Section 304-B of IPC and Section 113B of the Indian Evidence Act, 1872 (IEA) as under: (i) Section 304-B of IPC must be interpreted keeping in mind the legislative intent to curb the social evil of bride burning and dowry demand; (ii) The prosecution must at first establish the existence of the necessary ingredients for constituting an offence under Section 304-B of IPC. Once these ingredients are satisfied, the rebuttable presumption of causality, provided under Section 113-B of IEA operates against the accused;

(iii) The phrase 'soon before' as appearing in Section 304-B of IPC cannot be construed to mean 'immediately before'. The prosecution must establish existence of 'proximate and live link' between the cruelty or harassment for dowry demand by the husband or his relatives and the consequential death of the victim.

55. In *Gurmeet Singh v. State of Punjab*, 2021 SCC OnLine SC 403, a three-judge bench of the Supreme Court of India issued guidelines for trial in dowry death cases. The bench comprised of:

A.  N.V. Ramana, Uday Umesh Lalit and A.M. Khanwilkar, JJ.
B.  N.V. Ramana, Sanjay Kishan Kaul and Surya Kant, JJ.
C.  N.V. Ramana, Surya Kant and Aniruddha Bose, JJ.
D.  N.V. Ramana, L. Nageswara Rao and Hemant Gupta, JJ.

56.  In which of the following provisions is the term 'dowry' defined ?

A.  Section 2 of the Dowry Prohibition Act, 1961.
B.  Section 3 of the Dowry Prohibition Act, 1961.
C.  Section 498A of the Indian Penal Code, 1860.
D.  Section 304B of the Indian Penal Code, 1860.

57.  *"The presumption as to dowry death provided under Section 113B of the Indian Evidence Act, 1872 is a 'shall' presumption."* The given statement is:

A.  True.
B.  False.
C.  Neither true nor false as the application of the presumption is a matter of discretion of court.
D.  Neither true nor false as the application of the presumption depends on the facts of the case.

58.  Whether the demand for dowry was 'soon before' the death of the alleged victim of dowry death for establishing the offence under Section 304-B of the Indian Penal Code, 1860 is determined by the court on the basis of:

A.  The length of time between demand of dowry and death.
B.  The gravity of demand of dowry, including the existence of burns of injuries inflicted

while making such demand.

C.  The length of marriage of the victim and the accused.
D.  The totality of circumstances of each case, without relying on any straight jacket formula.

59.  In order to establish that the accused has committed an offence under Section 304-B of the Indian Penal Code, 1860, the prosecution is required to prove that the death of the victim occurring 'otherwise than under normal circumstances':

A.  Is either homicidal or suicidal death.
B.  Is accidental death only.
C.  May be homicidal or suicidal or accidental death.
D.  Is suicidal death only.

60.  The words 'soon before' in Section 304-B of the Indian Penal Code, 1860, are not interpreted as 'immediately before' because:

A.  A criminal statute is to be interpreted strictly.
B.  Section 304-B of the Indian Penal Code, 1860 is to be read with the presumption under Section 113B of the Indian Evidence Act, 1872.
C.  Once these ingredients are satisfied, the rebuttable presumption of causality under

Section 113-B of the Indian Evidence Act, 1872 operates against the accused.

   D. The legislative intent of Section 304-B of the Indian Penal Code, 1860 is to curb the social evil of bride burning and dowry demand.

XI. To every State whose land territory is at any place washed by the sea, international law attaches a corresponding portion of maritime territory... International law does not say to a State: "You are entitled to claim territorial waters if you want them". No maritime State can refuse them. International law imposes upon a maritime State, certain obligations and confers upon it certain rights arising out of the sovereignty which it exercises over its maritime territory. The possession of this territory is not optional, not dependent upon the will of the State, but compulsory. In the ninth edition of Oppenheim's International Law, the nationality of ships in the high seas has been referred to in paragraph 287, wherein it has been observed that the legal order on the high seas is based primarily on the rule of International Law which requires every vessel sailing the high seas to possess the nationality of, and to fly the flag of, one State, whereby a vessel and persons on board the vessel are subjected to the law of the State of the flag and in general subject to its exclusive jurisdiction. In paragraph 291 of the aforesaid discourse, the learned author has defined the scope of flag jurisdiction to mean that jurisdiction in the high seas is dependent upon the Maritime Flag under which vessels sail, because no State can extend its territorial jurisdiction to the high seas. Of course, the aforesaid principle is subject to the right of 'hot pursuit', which is an exception to the exclusiveness of the flag jurisdiction over ships on the high seas in certain special cases.

61. A Coastal State, subject to the obligations imposed by International Law, has sovereignty over its:

   A. Territorial waters, the seabed and subsoil underlying such waters, and the air space above them.
   B. Territorial waters, the seabed and subsoil underlying such waters.
   C. Territorial waters only.
   D. Territorial waters and the air space above them.

62. Which provision of the United Nations Convention on the Law of the Sea 1982 (UNCLOS) makes an express declaration that: *"No State may validly purport to subject any part of the high seas to its sovereignty."* ?

   A. Article 86 (B) Article 87

(C) Article 88 (D) Article 89

63. According to Article 94(7) of the United Nations Convention on the Law of the Sea 1982 (UNCLOS), in the event of a marine casualty or incident of navigation on the high seas involving a ship flying a State's flag and causing loss of life or serious injury to nationals of another State, which of the following shall be the duty of the Flag State?

   A. To conform to generally accepted international regulations, procedures and practices and to take any steps which may be necessary to mitigate the damage so caused.
   B. To cause an inquiry to be held by or before suitably qualified person(s) into such

casualty or incident.

   C. To investigate the matter and, if appropriate, take any action necessary to remedy the situation.
   D. To assume jurisdiction under its internal law over such casualty or incident in respect of its administrative, technical and social implications.

64. Territorial waters are not only 'territory' but also a compulsory to the coastal state.

    A.  Liability (B) Equitable interest

    (C) Appurtenance (D) Trust

65. The right of 'hot pursuit', which has been codified in Article 111 United Nations Convention

    on the Law of the Sea 1982 (UNCLOS) recognises that:

    A.  A vessel, if it has committed a violation of the laws of a foreign State while in that State's sovereign or territorial waters, may be pursued onto the high seas.
    B.  A vessel, if it has committed a violation of the provisions of the UNCLOS while in that State's sovereign or territorial waters, may be pursued onto the high seas.
    C.  A vessel, if it has committed a violation of the laws of a foreign State while in that State's sovereign or territorial waters, may be pursued onto the foreign State's sovereign or territorial waters.
    D.  A vessel, if it has committed a violation of the laws of a foreign State while in that State's sovereign or territorial waters, may be pursued onto a third State's sovereign or territorial waters.

66. In which of the following judgments, the Supreme Court of India has opined that "sovereignty is not 'given', but it is only asserted"?

    A.  State of Tamil Nadu v. Mariya Anton Vijay, (2015) 9 SCC 294.
    B.  Great Eastern Shipping Co. Ltd. v. State of Karnataka, (2020) 3 SCC 354.
    C.  Republic of Italy through Ambassador v. Union of India, (2013) 4 SCC 721.
    D.  Sabeeha Faikage v. Union of India, (2013) 1 SCC 262.

XII. Sections 31 to 35 of Chapter III of the Indian Contract Act, 1872 deals with contingent contracts and Section 36 deals with contingent agreements. A contingent contract is one where the liability to perform the promise depends upon some collateral event which may or may not happen. A contract of insurance is an example of a contingent contract, where the liability of the insurer depends upon the occurrence of the event, viz. damage or destruction arising out of fire. Life insurance in a broader sense comprises any contract in which one party agrees to pay a given sum upon happening of a particular event contingent upon duration of human life, in consideration of the immediate payment of a smaller sum or certain equivalent periodical payments by another. The event may be certain but it's happening in a specific manner or within a particular time would be uncertain. A contract of indemnity to make good the loss arising out of the conduct of the promisor is a contract contingent upon the act of a party. Such condition may be express or may also be implied into a contract. A contract for storage of potatoes in a cold storage cooling system was held subject to an implied condition that it could be performed only when there was continuous electric supply. But where there is a document embodying the terms of a contract, it is not permissible to imply therein a condition if that will be inconsistent with its express terms.

67. Which of the following is not correct about the nature of contingent contract?

    A.  A contract contingent upon the happening of an event can be enforced after that event occurs.
    B.  A contract contingent upon the happening of an event can be enforced even before that event occurs.
    C.  If the event becomes impossible, the contract becomes void.
    D.  The parties are under no obligation till the happening of that event unless there is a term requiring the parties to make effort to make that event happen.

68. 'A' agrees to pay 'B' a sum of money if a certain cruise does not return. The cruise is sunk. Based on the given facts, which of the following statement is correct?

    A. The contract can be enforced when the cruise sinks.
    B. Sinking of cruise has no relevance for validity of contract.
    C. The contract cannot be enforced when the cruise sinks.
    D. The condition is impossible.

69. Which of the following is correct regarding a contingent contract?

    A. No contract comes into existence until the contingency occurs.
    B. One party cannot assume an immediate unilateral obligation subject to a condition.
    C. The parties cannot enter into an immediately binding contract; and either the operation of the contract is made to depend upon the happening of the specified event.
    D. All contingent contracts are void.

70. 'X' promises to pay 'Y' a sum of money if a certain ship returns within a year. Based on the given facts, which of the following statement is not correct?

    A. The contract becomes void if the ship is burnt within the year.
    B. The contract depends upon returning or non-returning of the ship.
    C. The contract may be enforced if the ship returns within the year.
    D. The contract cannot be enforced if the ship returns within the year.

71. 'A' agrees to pay 'Z' an amount of ` 2 lakhs if 'Z' marries 'B'. 'B' was dead at the time of the said agreement between 'A' and 'Z'. Based on the given facts, which of the following statement is correct?

    A. The agreement is valid.
    B. The enforceability of agreement does not depend on the existence of 'B'.
    C. The agreement is void.
    D. The event is possible in its nature.

72. Which of the following statement correctly describes the difference between wagering agreements and contingent contracts?

    A. Wagering agreements are void and contingent contracts are valid.
    B. Wagering agreements are valid and contingent contracts are void.
    C. Wagering agreements and contingent contracts are valid.
    D. Wagering agreements and contingent contracts are void.

XIII. Supreme Court of India has pointed out that there are not less than 100 instances under the Income Tax Act, 1961, where in the event of amalgamation, the method of treatment of a particular subject matter is expressly indicated in the provisions of the Act. In some instances, amalgamation results in withdrawal of a special benefit (such as an area exemption under Section 80IA) - because it is entity or unit specific. In the case of carry forward of losses and profits, a nuanced approach has been indicated. All these provisions support the idea that the enterprise or the undertaking, and the business of the amalgamated company continues. The beneficial treatment, in the form of set-off, deductions (in proportion to the period the transferee was in existence, vis-à-vis the transfer to the transferee company); carry forward of loss, depreciation, all bear out that under the Act, (a) the business-including the rights, assets and liabilities of the transferor company do not cease, but continue; (b) by deeming fiction-through several provisions of the Act, the treatment of various issues, is such that the transferee is deemed to carry on the enterprise as that of the transferor.

73. Consider the given statements:

I. Amalgamation is the merger of one or more companies with another company.
II. Amalgamation may be the merger of two or more companies to form a new company.
III. The amalgamating company integrates with amalgamated company and the former is dissolved without winding up.

Choose the correct answer from the Code given below:
(A) Only (I) and (II) are true. (B) Only (II) and (III) are true.
(C) Only (I) and (III) are true. (D) (I), (II) and (III) are true.

74. On amalgamation of a company,

    A. There is transfer of capital assets from amalgamating company to amalgamated company and therefore capital gain can arise in the hands of the amalgamating company.
    B. There is transfer of capital assets from the amalgamating company to amalgamated company and hence capital gain can arise in the hands of the shareholders of the amalgamating company.
    C. Succession of capital assets of the amalgamating company by the amalgamated company does not result in transfer as defined in Section 47 of the Income Tax Act and hence no capital gain arises.
    D. All are incorrect.

75. In case of amalgamation,

    A. Amalgamated company can set off the losses of the amalgamating company, if conditions of Income Tax Act, 1961 are complied with.
    B. New company can claim depreciation on capital assets in the year of transfer on pro-rata basis.
    C. New company can carry forward unabsorbed depreciation.
    D. All are true.

76. Consider the given statements:

I. In case of amalgamation, transferee-company can claim deduction for expenditure incurred on amalgamation.
II. Any cessation of liability of amalgamating company shall be taxed in the hands of the amalgamated company.

Choose the correct answer from the Code given below:
(A) Both (I) and (II) are true. (B) Only (I) is true.
(C) Only (II) is true. (D) Both (I) and (II) are untrue.

77. Which of the following is true?

    A. The accumulated loss of the amalgamating company shall be deemed to be the loss of the amalgamated company for the previous year in which the amalgamation was effected.
    B. The amalgamated company can claim all deductions under Section 80 of Income

Tax Act, 1961 including unit specific deductions.

   C.  The accumulated loss of the amalgamating company shall not be deemed to be the loss of the amalgamated company.

   D.  All are incorrect.

78.  Consider the given statements:

I.  On amalgamation, the business of the transferor company does not cease, but is deemed to continue.

II.  Under various provisions of the Income Tax Act, transferee is deemed to carry on the enterprise as that of the transferor.

Choose the correct answer from the Code given below:
(A) Both (I) and (II) are true. (B) Only (I) is true.
(C) Only (II) is true. (D) Both (I) and (II) are untrue.

XIV.  The Supreme Court of India in a *Suo Motu* Writ Petition *In Re: Distribution of Essential Supplies and Services During Pandemic,* [Writ Petition (Civil) No. 3 of 2021], analyzed the power of judicial review over the management of the COVID-19 pandemic in India. The Union of India has highlighted a few concerns as: The executive is battling an unprecedented crisis and the government needs discretion to formulate policy in larger interest and its wisdom should be trusted; The current vaccine policy conforms to Articles 14 and 21 of the Constitution, and requires no interference from the courts as the executive has room for free play in the joints while dealing with a pandemic of this magnitude; Judicial review over executive policies is permissible only on account of manifest arbitrariness. No interference from judicial proceedings is called for when the executive is operating on expert medical and scientific opinion to tackle a medical crisis; and any over-zealous judicial intervention, though well-meaning, in the absence of expert advice or administrative experience may lead to unintended circumstances where the executive is left with little room to explore innovative solutions. The court clarified that in the context of the public health emergency, the executive has been given a wider margin in enacting measures which ordinarily may have violated the liberty of individual. The judiciary has also recognized that Constitutional scrutiny is transformed during such public health emergencies and noted the complex role of the government in battling public health emergencies in following words: ...*While this court should guard with firmness every right appertaining to life, liberty or property as secured to the individual by the Supreme Law of the Land, it is of the last importance that it should not invade the domain of local authority except when it is plainly necessary to do so in order to enforce that law. But even in a pandemic, the Constitution cannot be put away and forgotten and a public health emergency does not give Governors and other public officials carte blanche to disregard the Constitution for as long as the medical problem persists. ...the courts should expect policies that more carefully account for Constitutional rights.* The court stated that separation of powers is a part of the basic structure of the Constitution of India. However, this separation of powers does not result in courts lacking jurisdiction in conducting a judicial review of these policies.

79.  Which of the following statements is untrue?

   A.  Policy-making lays in the sole domain of the executive.
   B.  The power of judicial review may be exercised on public health policies.
   C.  Separation of powers restricts the power of judicial review on public health policies.
   D.  Policy-making should be in conformity with the fundamental rights.

80.  Soliciting constitutional justification for executive policies in managing a public health

crisis during pandemic appears to be:

    A.  Necessary function of the court. (B) Discretionary power of the court.

(C) Not within the ambit of judicial review. (D) Unnecessary interference from the court.

81.  In the above excerpt, the Union of India opposed judicial intervention in apprehension of circumstances restricting the scope for the executive to explore solutions. The said argument was supported on the ground that :

    A.  The judges are not public health experts, therefore in the absence of expert advice, it would be an undesirable intervention.
    B.  The executive needs room for free play while dealing with pandemic.
    C.  Constitutional rights are suspended during a pandemic.
    D.  Both (A) and (B).

82.  Consider the following statements:

I.  An intrusion by the judiciary in the domain of the executive is prohibited under the separation of powers principle, except when it is necessary to do so in order to enforce the express provisions of the Constitution of India.
II.  An intrusion by the judiciary in the domain of the executive is allowed when it is necessary to do so in order to safeguard the rights relating to life, liberty or property as secured to the individual by the Constitution of India.

Choose the correct answer from the code given below.
(A) Both (I) and (II) are true. (B) Both (I) and (II) are untrue.
(C) (I) is true and (II) is untrue. (D) (II) is true and (I) is untrue.

83.  In the case of *In Re: Distribution of Essential Supplies and Services During Pandemic*, the Supreme Court of India examined the constitutional validity of Central Government's policy regarding vaccine procurement and distribution among different categories of the population. Such policy is known as:

    A.  Vaccination Distribution Policy. (B) Liberalized Vaccination Policy.

(C) Central Vaccination Distribution Policy. (D) None of the above.

84.  Public health is a subject under of the Seventh Schedule of the Constitution.

    A.  Entry 6 of List II (State List) (B) Entry 36 of List II (State List)

(C) Entry 81 of List I (Union List) (D) Entry 29 of List III (Concurrent List)

XV.  The right to clean and healthy environment has been recognized as a fundamental right under Article 21 of the Constitution of India. Article 48-A imposes a duty upon the State to endeavour to protect and improve the environment and safeguard the forests and wildlife of the Country. In addition to this, India is also a party to international treaties, agreements and conferences and has committed itself to sustainable development and growth. This legal framework indicates that sustainable development must remain at the heart of any development policy implemented by the state. It is essential to strike the right balance between environmental conservation and protection on one hand, and the right to development on the other, while articulating the doctrine of sustainable development. We may add that in our opinion conservation and development need not be viewed as binaries, but as complementary strategies that weave into one another. In other words, conservation of nature must be viewed as part of development and not as a factor stultifying development.

85. Which of the following provisions contain the fundamental duty to protect and improve the natural environment?

(A) 51A(h) (B) 51A(g) (C) 51A(f) (D) 51A(d)

86. Under which of the following provisions can Union legislature enact laws for giving effect to international agreements?

A. Article 251 (B) Article 252

(C) Article 253 (D) Article 254

87. By which of the following Constitution Amendment Act were Entries 17A and 17B inserted in List III of the Seventh Schedule of the Constitution of India?

A. Constitution (Fortieth Amendment) Act, 1976
B. Constitution (Forty Second Amendment) Act, 1976
C. Constitution (Forty Fourth Amendment) Act, 1978
D. Constitution (Forty Sixth Amendment) Act, 1982

88. Which of the following judgments of the Supreme Court of India does not deal with sustainable development?

A. Karnataka Industrial Area Development Board v. C. Kenchappa, (2006) 6 SCC 371.
B. Tata Housing Development Co. Ltd. v. Aalok Jagga, (2020) 15 SCC 784.
C. Manorama Sachan v. Lucknow Development Authority, (2005) 9 SCC 425.
D. Maharashtra Land Development Corporation v. State of Maharashtra, (2011) 15 SCC 616.

89. Which of the following depicts the most appropriate response regarding Public Trust Doctrine?

A. That resources like sea, waters, forests are extremely important to the masses and

therefore it would be unjustified to make them subjects of private ownership.

B. The people of the country have a fundamental duty to protect the environment.
C. Right to clean environment is a fundamental right.
D. All of the above.

90. Which of the following doctrines is/are part of environmental jurisprudence in India?

A. Polluter Pays Principle (B) Precautionary Principle

(C) Both (A) and (B) (D) Sovereign Immunity Principle

XVI. In cases where the evidence is of a circumstantial nature, the circumstances which lead to the conclusion of guilt should be in the first instance fully established, and all the facts so established should be consistent only with the hypothesis of the guilt of the accused. Again, the circumstances should be of a conclusive nature and tendency and they should be such as to exclude every hypothesis but the one proposed to be proved. In other words, there must be a chain of evidence so far complete as not to leave any reasonable ground for a conclusion consistent with the innocence of the accused and it must be shown that within all human probability the act must have been committed by the accused.

91. When a person does an act with some intention other than that which the character and circumstances of the act suggest, the burden of proving that intention is:

    A. Upon that person who conceive such intention.
    B. Not upon that person who conceive such intention.
    C. Upon prosecution irrespective to the fact who conceived such intention.
    D. Not clear under the provisions of the Indian Evidence Act, 1872.

92. Where in a criminal case there is conflict between presumption of innocence and any

other presumption, in such situation which presumption shall prevail?

    A. Presumption of guilty (B) Presumption of innocence

(C) Mix Presumption (D) No presumption

93. Where the evidence is of a circumstantial nature, the circumstances from which the conclusion of guilt is to be drawn should be:

    A. Partially established (B) Fully established

(C) Reasonably established (D) Initially established

94. An admissibility of circumstantial evidence against the accused requires a chain of evidence which:

    A. Does not leave any reasonable ground for a conclusion consistent with the innocence of the accused.
    B. Does not leave any reasonable ground for a conclusion inconsistent with the innocence of the accused.
    C. Must be such as to show that within all human probability the act must have been done by the accused.
    D. Both (A) and (C).

95. When a murder charge is to be proved solely on circumstantial evidence, a presumption of innocence of the accused must have a role.

    A. Common (B) Reasonable

(C) Dominant (D) Minimum

96. Which provision of the Indian Evidence Act, 1872 provides regarding the burden of proving that case of accused comes within general exceptions of the Indian Penal Code, 1860?

A.  Section 104 (B) Section 105

(C) Section 106 (D) Section 107

XVII. On repeal of the Juvenile Justice Act, 2000 and on the enforcement of the Juvenile Justice Act, 2015, the procedure to be followed when a claim of juvenility is raised before any court, other than a Board is stipulated under Section 9(2) and (3). The same reads as "In case a person alleged to have committed an offence claims before a court other than a Board, that the person is a child or was a child on the date of commission of the offence, or if the court itself is of the opinion that the person was a child on the date of commission of the offence, the said court shall make an inquiry, take such evidence as may be necessary (but not an affidavit) to determine the age of such person, and shall record a finding on the matter, stating the age of the person as nearly as may be: *Provided* that such a claim may be raised before any court and it shall be recognized at any stage, even after final disposal of the case, and such a claim shall be determined in accordance with the provisions contained in this Act and the rules made thereunder even if the person has ceased to be a child on or before the date of commencement of this Act. If the court finds that a person has committed an offence and was a child on the date of commission of such offence, it shall forward the child to the Board for passing appropriate orders and the sentence, if any, passed by the court shall be deemed to have no effect."

97.  From which of the following dates Juvenile Justice Act, 2015 was implemented?

A.  January 16, 2015 (B) January 15, 2016

(C) February 16, 2016 (D) February 15, 2015

98.  'A' is accused of having committed an offence on January 1, 2022. He attained the age of 16 on March 31, 2022. On the date of hearing, he claimed that on the date of commission of the offence, he was a child. Which of the following statement is true?

A.  'A' can raise the plea of juvenility since he was child on the date of commission of the offence.
B.  'A' cannot be allowed to raise the plea of juvenility.
C.  For raising the plea of juvenility, the age on the date of trial is considered and not the age on the date of commission of offence.
D.  All are true.

99.  Which of the following statements is true, if the plea of juvenility is raised before the court?

A.  The Court can decide the plea of juvenility only on the basis of the affidavit of the

claimant.

B.  The Court shall get the enquiry conducted by collector of the district.
C.  The Court shall take such evidence as it considers necessary and decide the age of the claimant.
D.  Both (A) and (B) are true.

100.  'A' is accused of committing an offence on a given day. He claims that he was child on such day. Court conducts an enquiry and records a finding that he was child on the date of offence. Which of the following statements holds good?

A. The Court is bound to try the entire case and decide whether the claimant has committed the offence.
B. The order of conviction passed by the Court after recording finding that the accused

is a child, is valid.

C. The Court shall forward the matter to Juvenile Justice Board for decision and appropriate orders.
D. The Court shall set the accused free.

101. The Juvenile Justice Act, 2015 contemplates certain children to be kept in special homes. Which of the following children can be kept in special homes?

A. Orphaned children (B) Abused children

(C) Neglected children (D) Children in conflict with law

102. Which of the following is referred to as 'Orphan' in the Juvenile Justice Act, 2015?

A. A child who is without a biological parent
B. A child who is without an adoptive parent
C. A child who is without a legal guardian
D. All the above

XVIII. Drinking water is of primary importance in any country. In fact, India is a party to the Resolution of the UNO passed during the United Nations Water Conference which reads as under:

"All people, whatever their stage of development and their social and economic conditions, have the right to have access to drinking water in quantum and of a quality equal to their basic needs." Thus, the right to access to drinking water is fundamental to life and there is a duty on the State under Article 21 to provide clean drinking water to its citizens. There is, therefore, need to take into account the right to a healthy environment along with the right to sustainable development and balance them. Competing Human Rights to healthy environment and sustainable development.

103. In which of the following cases the Supreme Court held that water is the basic need for the survival of human beings and is part of right of life and Human Rights as enshrined in Article 21 of the Constitution of India?

A. Bandhua Mukti Morcha v. Union of India (1984) 3 SCC 161
B. Narmada Bachao Andolan v. Union of India (2000) 7 SCALE 34
C. State of Madhya Pradesh v. Centre for Environment Protection Research and Development 2020 SCC OnLine SC 687
D. M.C. Mehta v. Union of India (2004) 12 SCC 118

104. Which of the following Courts was the first court to develop the concept of right to healthy

environment as part of the Fundamental Right to life?

A. Philippine Supreme Court (B) Supreme Court of India

(C) European Court of Justice (D) Supreme Court of South Africa

105.  In today's emerging Jurisprudence, Environmental rights which encompass a group of collective rights are described as:

    A.  First generation rights (B) Second generation rights

(C) Third generation rights (D) Fourth generation rights

106.  When was the first United Nations Water Conference held?

(A) 1975 (B) 1976 (C) 1977 (D) 1978

107.  The resolution of the UNO passed during the United Nations Water Conference as- All people, whatever their stage of development and their social and economic conditions, have the right to have access to drinking water:

    A.  In quantum equal to their basic needs
    B.  In quantum according to their age
    C.  In quantum according to their natural needs
    D.  In quantum according to their climatic conditions

108.  The right to access drinking water is a:

    A.  Statutory Right (B) Fundamental Right

(C) Community Right (D) Individual Privilege

XIX.  If a tax is ultra vires or unconstitutional then the party is entitled to have a refund of it from the government whether it has been paid under protest or not. This Court has held that the payment of tax which is without authority of law is payment made under a mistake within the meaning of Section 72 of the Indian Contract Act. Then, in such a case, question would arise, whether the government to whom the payment had been made by mistake must repay it. Thus, the principle of restitution or repayment of the tax simpliciter has been considered in light of the doctrine of unlawful enrichment. The doctrine envisages that when the State collects a tax from the tax-payer without authority of law, but if the taxpayer has already passed on the burden of the tax money paid by him to the State to someone else and has recouped the money then the taxpayer is not entitled to ask for the restitution from the State the money paid by him as unauthorized tax. In such circumstances, the State cannot be asked to refund the tax money to the taxpayer on the principle of unlawful enrichment.

109.  Doctrine of Unjust Enrichment implies:

    A.  Obtaining benefit from another (which is not a gift) without legal justification
    B.  Restoration of the benefits obtained without legal justification
    C.  Neither (A) nor (B)
    D.  Both (A) and (B)

110.  Doctrine of Unjust Enrichment is applicable to:

    A.  Contractual Matters (B) Tax Matters

(C) Both (A) and (B) (D) None of these

111. A business entity can claim refund of tax on the ground of unjust enrichment in which of the following cases?

    A. When the tax has been levied without the authority of law and the burden of tax is borne by the business entity.
    B. When the tax has been levied without the authority of law and the burden of tax has been passed on to the consumer.
    C. When levy of tax is under the authority of law and the business entity has not passed the burden to the consumer.
    D. Both (A) and (C)

112. When can tax be declared as unconstitutional?

    A. If tax has been levied without the authority of law.
    B. If the legislature does not have legislative competence to levy that tax.
    C. Both (A) and (B)
    D. When the assessment of tax by assessing officer is contrary to facts and evidence

on record.

113. In which of the following cases, challenge to constitutionality of the Goods and Service Tax (Compensation to States) Act, 2017 on the ground of lack of legislative competence was rejected?

    A. Union of India v. Mohit Minerals Pvt. Ltd. (2019) 2 SCC 599.
    B. Sudhir Kumar Atrey v. Union of India (2022) 1 SCC 352.
    C. Hindustan Construction Co. Limited v. Union of India (2020) 17 SCC 324.
    D. Union of India v. A. Shainamol 2021 SCC OnLine SC 262.

114. Additional tax, in the form of tax on tax, for a specified purpose is called:

    A. Cess (B) Fee (C) Tax (D) None of the above

XX. The International Court of Justice recalls that, pursuant to Article 41 of its Statute, it has the power to indicate provisional measures when irreparable prejudice could be caused to rights which are the subject of judicial proceedings or when the alleged disregard of such rights may entail irreparable consequences. However, this power will be exercised only if there is urgency, in the sense that there is a real and imminent risk that irreparable prejudice will be caused to the rights claimed before the Court gives its final decision. The condition of urgency is met when the acts susceptible of causing irreparable prejudice can "occur at any moment" before the Court makes a final decision on the case. The Court must therefore consider whether such a risk exists at this stage of the proceedings. The Court is not called upon, for the purposes of its decision on the Request for the indication of provisional measures, to establish the existence of breaches of obligations under the Genocide Convention, but to determine whether the circumstances require the indication of provisional measures for the protection of the right found to be plausible. Having determined that Ukraine can plausibly assert a right under the Genocide Convention and that there is a link between this right and the provisional measures requested, the Court then considers whether irreparable prejudice could be caused to this right and whether there is urgency, in the sense that there is a real and imminent risk that irreparable prejudice will be caused to this right before the Court gives its final decision.

115. Under what statutory authority did the court pass the 'provisional measures' against the Russian Federation?

A. Charter of the United Nations 1945
B. Statute of the International Court of Justice 1945
C. Genocide Convention, 1948
D. None of the above

116. What 'irreparable prejudice' is being talked about in the above paragraph?

A. Violation of the Genocide Convention by Russian Federation.
B. Special military operations carried out against the Ukraine.
C. Violation of Humanitarian laws during the armed conflict by Russian Federation.
D. All of the above

117. The reason behind the Russian-Ukraine crisis is:

A. The violation of Geneva Convention of the Refugees 1951
B. The violation of the Agreement between Confederation of Independent States and Europe
C. Threat or use of force contrary to the Purpose and Principles of the United Nations Charter
D. Neither (A) nor (B)

118. If one of the two parties to the dispute fails to appear before the Court during the oral proceedings, the other party may call upon the court to decide the matter in favour of its claim. Which of the following provision provides for this?

A. Article 41 of the Statute of the ICJ (B) Article 51 of the Statute of the ICJ

(C) Article 52 of the Statute of the ICJ (D) Article 53 of the Statute of the ICJ

119. Under which of the following provisions, Ukraine sought jurisdiction to appear before the Court?

A. Article 36 of the Statute of the ICJ (B) Article IX of the Genocide Convention

(C) Both (A) and (B) (D) Neither (A) nor (B)

120. The Russian Federation, in the current dispute submitted to the court, the defence of Article 51 of the UN Charter. What is defence of Article 51?

A. Self-defence (B) *Force Majure*

(C) Consent (D) *Pacta sunt servanda*

**SPACE FOR ROUGH WORK**

# ANSWER KEY TO PG QUESTION PAPER 2022

## CLAT 2022

### FINAL ANSWER KEY – P.G.

| Ques No. | Correct Answer | Ques No. | Correct Answer | Ques No. | Correct Answer |
|---|---|---|---|---|---|
| 1 | A | 41 | B | 81 | D |
| 2 | B | 42 | A | 82 | A |
| 3 | A | 43 | D | 83 | B |
| 4 | A | 44 | B | 84 | A |
| 5 | B | 45 | B | 85 | B |
| 6 | A | 46 | D | 86 | C |
| 7 | A | 47 | C | 87 | B |
| 8 | D | 48 | B | 88 | C |
| 9 | A | 49 | D | 89 | A |
| 10 | C | 50 | B | 90 | C |
| 11 | A | 51 | C | 91 | A |
| 12 | A | 52 | C | 92 | B |
| 13 | C | 53 | A | 93 | B |
| 14 | A | 54 | B | 94 | D |
| 15 | B | 55 | C | 95 | C |
| 16 | C | 56 | A | 96 | B |
| 17 | A | 57 | A | 97 | B |
| 18 | C | 58 | D | 98 | A |
| 19 | D | 59 | C | 99 | C |
| 20 | B | 60 | D | 100 | C |
| 21 | A | 61 | A | 101 | D |
| 22 | B | 62 | D | 102 | D |
| 23 | C | 63 | B | 103 | B |
| 24 | C | 64 | C | 104 | B |
| 25 | B | 65 | A | 105 | C |
| 26 | A | 66 | C | 106 | C |
| 27 | D | 67 | B | 107 | A |
| 28 | C | 68 | A | 108 | B |
| 29 | D | 69 | A | 109 | D |
| 30 | D | 70 | D | 110 | C |
| 31 | D | 71 | C | 111 | A |
| 32 | C | 72 | A | 112 | C |
| 33 | A | 73 | D | 113 | A |
| 34 | B | 74 | C | 114 | A |
| 35 | A | 75 | D | 115 | B |
| 36 | D | 76 | A | 116 | D |
| 37 | C | 77 | A | 117 | C |
| 38 | C | 78 | A | 118 | D |
| 39 | A | 79 | C | 119 | C |

Enter Caption

# CHAPTER NINE

# REFERENCES


1. The Hindu Newspaper

1. https://www.mbarendezvous.com/easy-reading-comprehension-passages/

3. Ignited Minds: unleashing the power within India; Dr APJ Abdul Kalam; Pg. 40-43; Penguin Books Ltd.

4. Wuthering Heights by Emily Bronte; Chapter-I; Page- 1&2

5. *David Copperfield* by Charles Dickens; Fingerprint! Publishing (17 February 2017), India

6. https://www.grammarbank.com/beginners-reading-comprehension-7.html

7. Confronting Xi: India should engage both the Dalai Lama and Taiwan July 7, 2021, 10:29 PM IST TOI Edit in TOI Editorials, India. https://timesofindia.indiatimes.com/blogs/toi-editorials/confronting-xi-india-should-engage-both-the-dalai-lama-and-taiwan/

8. https://www.jagranjosh.com/articles/ugc-net-reading-comprehension-questions-with-answers-1560863903-1

9. https://static.collegedekho.com/media/uploads/2022/06/20/ug-2022-qp_BgXhwlL.pdf

10. https://static.collegedekho.com/media/uploads/2022/06/20/pg-2022-qp_F7o3Qel.pdf

*GOOD LUCK!!!*

www.ingramcontent.com/pod-product-compliance
Lightning Source LLC
Chambersburg PA
CBHW060601120726
48002CB00010B/2772